Excel 2019 Functions

70 Top Excel Functions Made Easy

NATHAN GEORGE

Copyright © 2019 Nathan George

All rights reserved.

ISBN: 978-1796379945

The information given in this book is given in good faith and belief in its accuracy at the time of publication. The author and publishers disclaim any liability arising directly or indirectly from the use, or misuse, of the information contained in this book.

CONTENTS

Introduction 7
    Who Is This Book For? 7
    How to Use This Book 8
    Assumptions 8
    Practice Files 9

Chapter 1: How to Enter a Formula 10
    The Insert Function Dialog Box 11

Chapter 2: Lookup and Reference Functions 15
    VLOOKUP Function 16
    HLOOKUP Function 19
    MATCH Function 22
    CHOOSE Function 26
    TRANSPOSE Function 29
    ADDRESS function 31
    FORMULATEXT Function 34
    COLUMNS Function 36
    ROWS Function 37
    INDEX Function 39
        INDEX Function - Array Form 39
        INDEX Function - Reference form 42

Chapter 3: Logical Functions 45
    IF Function 46
        Nested IF Functions 49
        Advanced IF Functions 50
    IFS Function 53
    SWITCH Function 57
    IFERROR Function 59

AND Function 61
OR Function 64
Chapter 4: Math Functions **67**
SUM Function 68
SUMIF Function 71
SUMIFS Function 74
AGGREGATE Function 77
MOD Function 81
RANDBETWEEN Function 82
ROUND Function 84
ROUNDUP Function 86
ROUNDDOWN Function 88
SQRT Function 90
Chapter 5: Statistical Functions **91**
COUNT Function 92
COUNTIF Function 94
COUNTIFS Function 98
COUNTA Function 101
COUNTBLANK Function 103
AVERAGE Function 105
AVERAGEIF Function 107
AVERAGEIFS Function 111
MAX, MIN, MEDIAN Functions 114
MAXIFS, MINIFS Functions 116
Chapter 6: Date and Time Functions **120**
Date Formats 121
DAY, MONTH, YEAR Functions 123
DATE Function 126
DATEDIF Function 131
DAYS Function 134
EDATE Function 136

DATEVALUE Function 138
NETWORKDAYS Function 140
NOW Function 142
TODAY Function 144
TIME Function 146

Chapter 7: Text Functions 148
FIND Function 150
   FINDB 151
CONCAT Function 152
TEXTJOIN Function 154
TRIM Function 157
UPPER, LOWER Functions 158
LEN Function 159
   LENB 159
MID Function 161
   MIDB 162
PROPER Function 163
LEFT, RIGHT Functions 164
   LEFTB, RIGHTB Functions 166

Chapter 8: Financial Functions 168
Definitions 169
PV Function 170
FV Function 173
NPV Function 176
PMT Function 179
SLN Function 181
SYD Function 183
DB Function 185
DDB Function 189

Afterword: Getting More Help with Functions 192
Appendix: Keyboard Shortcuts (Excel for Windows) 193

Glossary 196
Index 199
About The Author 201
Other Books by Author 202

INTRODUCTION

Excel 2019 Functions covers the most useful functions in each category of Excel functions based on how often they're used in common Excel tasks and specialized work. Functions can save you a lot of time and effort as they're predefined formulas only needing you to provide the input values. Functions help to reduce errors in your formulas as they are tried and tested. Also, knowing more of what tools are available to you in Excel enables you to create more robust designs for your solutions.

My *Excel 2019 Basics* book covered the most commonly used functions in everyday Excel tasks. *Excel 2019 Functions* goes beyond the basics and covers advanced functions like the IFS functions and other advanced functions for text manipulation, statistics, and finance. You also get to learn how to combine several functions in creating solutions for more complex problems.

Excel 2019 Functions covers each function in detail, including appropriate examples, in a concise and to the point manner. The aim is to provide you with solutions for your data as quickly as possible without needing to wade through a ton of text.

Who Is This Book For?

This book is for you if you want to learn more about Excel functions and if you need a functions companion guide when working with Excel. *Excel 2019 Functions* provides a treasure trove of ideas and solutions for better ways of approaching Excel problems.

This book assumes you have some basic knowledge of Excel. For brevity, foundational topics that have already been covered in my *Excel 2019 Basics* book have not been covered here again. If you need to brush up on the basics (or if you're completely new to Excel), then my *Excel 2019 Basics* book covers all the foundation knowledge you'll need.

The lessons in this book have been created using Excel 2019. However, if you have an earlier version of Excel, you'll find many of the lessons in this book relevant because many of the functions covered are available in prior versions of Excel.

The functions introduced in Excel 2019 are pointed out in the book. If you have a version of Excel earlier than 2010, the menu options and dialog boxes may look significantly different. However, the covered functions available in those versions will work in the same way.

How to Use This Book

Excel 2019 Functions has been designed as a reference manual or a companion guide that you have at hand as you work with Excel. You can read the chapters in sequential order or pick and choose which topics you want to cover. As much as possible, each function in this book has been covered as a standalone tutorial. A side effect of this is that there will be some repetition as it is not assumed that you're reading the chapters in chronological order.

Some examples use multi-function solutions, however, all functions used in the included examples are covered individually in the book. The functions have also been organized into categories to make it easier for you to find the right function for a specific problem you want to address.

Assumptions

The software and hardware assumptions made when writing this book is that you already have Excel installed on your computer and that you're working on the Windows platform (7, 8 or 10). If you are using Excel on a Mac, then substitute any Windows keyboard commands mentioned in the book for the Mac equivalent. All the features within Excel remain the same for both platforms.

If you're using Excel on a tablet or touchscreen device, again, simply substitute any keyboard commands mentioned in the book with the equivalent on your touchscreen device.

Practice Files

Downloadable Excel practice files have been provided to save you typing if you want to practice as you follow the examples in the book. All examples are fully detailed in the book, so the practice files are optional. You can practice by changing the data to view different results. You can also copy and use the predefined formulas in your own worksheets. Go to the following link to download the Excel examples in this book:

https://www.excelbytes.com/excel-functions-download

Notes:

- Type the URL in your Internet browser's address bar and press Enter to navigate to the download page. If you encounter an error, double-check that you have entered all characters in the URL correctly.

- The files have been zipped into one download. Windows 10 comes with the functionality to unzip files. If your OS does not have this functionality, you'll need to get a piece of software like WinZip or WinRAR to unzip the file.

- The files are Excel 2019 files so you will need to have Excel installed on your computer to open and use these files (preferably Excel 2013 and above).

- If you are having any problems downloading these files, please contact me at **support@excelbytes.com**. Include the title of this book in your email, and the practice files will be emailed directly to you.

CHAPTER 1: HOW TO ENTER A FORMULA

To insert a formula/function:

1. Click the cell where you want to display the result.
2. Click in the formula bar.
3. Enter your formula, starting your entry with the equal sign (=). This specifies that your entry is a formula and not a static value.

For example:

=SUM(A2:A10)

Tip: As much as possible, avoid typing cell references directly into the formula bar as it could introduce errors. Instead, enter the name of the formula and then open bracket, for example, enter **=SUM(**. Then select the cells you want for your argument in the worksheet itself, then enter the closing bracket.

The Insert Function Dialog Box

A second way you can enter a function is by using the **Insert Function** dialog box.

Click in the formula bar to place the cursor there and click the **Insert Function** command on the **Formulas** tab, or the Insert Function button next to the formula bar.

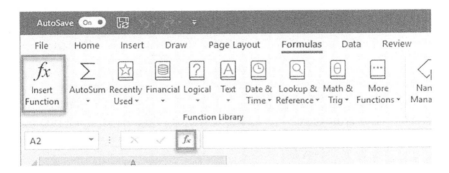

This will display the **Insert Function** dialog box. This dialog box provides the option to search for the function or select it from a category.

To search for the function, enter the name of the function in the **Search for a function** box. For example, if you were searching for the IF function you would enter IF in the search box and click **Go**. The **Select a function** list will display all the functions related to your search term.

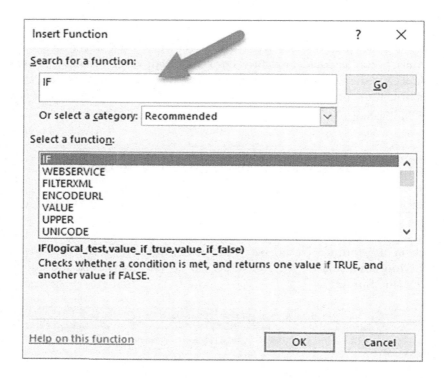

You can also use the **category** drop-down list to select a function if you know its category in Excel. For example, you can find the IF function in the **Logical** category.

If you have used a function recently it'll be listed in the **Most Recently Used** category.

EXCEL 2019 FUNCTIONS

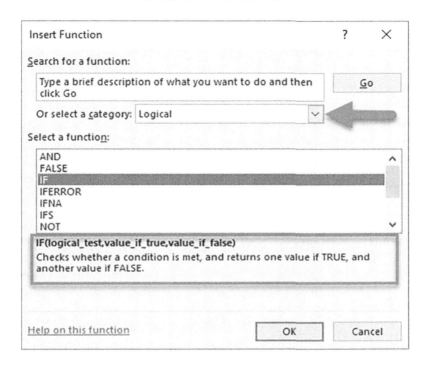

When you select a function on the list, you'll see the syntax for the function and a description of what the function does below the list.

Once you've selected the one you want, click **OK** to go to the **Functions Arguments** screen.

The Functions Arguments screen enables you to enter the arguments for the function. A function argument is a piece of data that the function needs in order to run.

The Functions Arguments screen is particularly useful if you are not familiar with a function because it provides a description of each argument, a preview of your entries, and the result returned by the function.

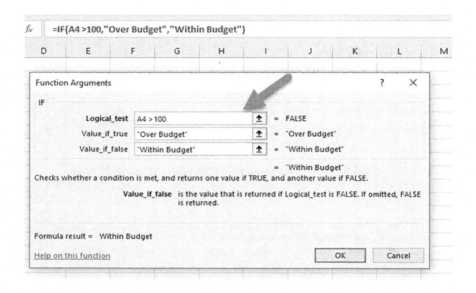

After entering the arguments, click **OK** and the formula will be inserted in the formula bar.

CHAPTER 2: LOOKUP AND REFERENCE FUNCTIONS

The Lookup and Reference functions can be found by clicking on the **Lookup & Reference** command button on the Formulas tab on the Ribbon. Excel provides many functions to enable you to look up one piece of data using another. Reference functions allow you to search for specific information or return certain information about your worksheet.

In this chapter, we'll cover functions that enable you to:
- Lookup data in a list, table, or range based on a lookup value.
- Transpose a column or row of data.
- Choose a value from a list, table, or range based on a search index.
- Return the address of a cell in your worksheet.
- Display the formula of a cell (rather than the return value).
- Return the number of rows or columns in a range.

VLOOKUP Function

The VLOOKUP function (vertical lookup) is the most commonly used lookup function in Excel. This is the updated version of the legacy LOOKUP function. The old LOOKUP function is still available in Excel for backward compatibility, but it is no longer recommended. Use VLOOKUP or HLOOKUP going forwards as they're more robust and better supported in the new versions of Excel.

VLOOKUP enables you to find one piece of information in a workbook based on another piece of information. For example, if you have a *Products* table, you can find and return the *Product Code* by providing the *Product Name* to the VLOOKUP function.

Syntax

VLOOKUP (lookup_value, table_array, col_index_num, [range_lookup])

Arguments

Argument	Description
Lookup_value	Required. What value are you searching for? This is the lookup value. Excel will look for a match for this value in the leftmost column of your chosen range. You can provide a value here or a cell reference.
Table_array	Required. What columns do you want to search? This is the lookup table containing the columns you want to include in your search e.g. A2:D10.
Col_index_num	Required. Which column contains the search result? Count from the first column to determine what this number should be, starting from 1.
Range_lookup	Optional. If you want an exact match, enter FALSE or 0 here. However, if an approximate match is OK then enter TRUE or 1. For TRUE, you would need to sort the leftmost column in ascending order for correct results. This is an optional argument and if left out it will default to TRUE.

EXCEL 2019 FUNCTIONS

Example

In the example below, we use VLOOKUP to find the *Price* and Reorder Level of a product by entering the *Product Name* in cell G2. The formula is in cell G3 and as you can see from the image below, it searches the table for *Dried Pears* and returns the price from the next column.

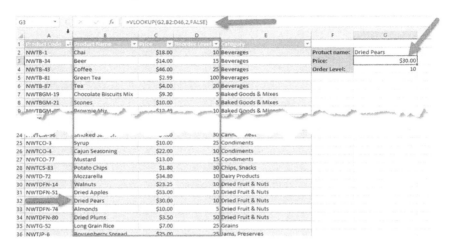

Formula Explanation

To look up the **Price** for Dried Pears the formula is:

=VLOOKUP(G2, B2:D46, 2, FALSE)

The function uses a lookup_value from cell **G2** to search a table_array which is **B2:D46**.

The col_index_num is **2** so it returns a value from the second column in the table_array, which is the **Price** column.

The range_lookup is **FALSE** meaning we want an exact match.

To look up the **Reorder Level** for Dried Pears we use the same formula and just change the column that contains the search result (**col_index_num**) to 3 so that it returns a value from the third row of the table array.

=VLOOKUP(G2, B2:D46, **3**, FALSE)

In this case, the VLOOKUP search for Dried Pears returns a Reorder Level of **10**.

EXCEL 2019 FUNCTIONS

HLOOKUP Function

The HLOOKUP function (horizontal lookup) searches for a value in the top row of a range or table and then returns a value in the same column from a row you specify in the range or table. The function carries out a horizontal search on the first column of the specified range for the lookup value (criteria). Then it uses the criteria to return another value from the same column but on a row below.

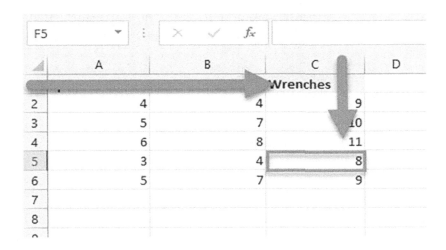

Use HLOOKUP when your lookup values are in a row at the top of a range or table, and you want to look down a specified number of rows. VLOOKUP, on the other hand, is suitable when your lookup values are in a column to the left of the data you want to search for.

Syntax

HLOOKUP(lookup_value, table_array, row_index_num, [range_lookup])

Arguments

Argument	Description
Lookup_value	Required. This is the value to be used as the lookup value and it should be in the first row of table_array. Lookup_value can be text, a value, or a reference.

Table_array	Required. This is a range, or table which contains the data being looked up. You can use cell references or a named range.
Row_index_num	Required. This is the row number from which you want the value returned counting from 1 from the first row of the range.
Range_lookup	Optional. This argument is to specify whether HLOOKUP should find an exact match or an approximate match. TRUE is for an approximate match while FALSE is for an exact match. If this argument is omitted, it'll default to TRUE.

Example

	A	B	C
1	Spanners	Bolts	Wrenches
2	4	4	9
3	5	7	10
4	6	8	11
5	3	4	8
6	5	7	9
7			

Using the data above, we get the following results using HLOOKUP to query the range:

=HLOOKUP("Bolts",A1:C6,6,FALSE)

Answer: 7

This is using "Bolts" as the lookup value to return a value on row 6 from the same column.

****

=HLOOKUP("Spanners",A1:C6,3,FALSE)

EXCEL 2019 FUNCTIONS

Answer: 5

This is using "Spanners" as the lookup value to return a value on row 3 from the same column.

****

=HLOOKUP("Wrenches",A1:C6,3)

Answer: 10

This is using "Wrenches" as the lookup value to return a value on row 3 from the same column.

MATCH Function

The MATCH function searches for a given item in a list and then returns the relative position of the item in the list. That means, MATCH tells you where in your list you can locate your value after you provide search parameters.

If MATCH cannot find an exact match, it will find the closest item to the lookup value. This can be useful in situations where you want to identify the cut-off point in a list of values.

For example, if the range A1:A5 has the values 10, 30, 26, 44, and 100, the formula =MATCH(44,A1:A5,0) will return 4, because 44 is the fourth item in the range.

MATCH is most useful when used as an argument in another function where you need to return the position of a specific item in your data as one of the arguments of the other function.

Syntax

MATCH(lookup_value, lookup_array, [match_type])

Arguments

Argument	Description
lookup_value	Required. This is the value that you want to match in your list. This argument can be a number, cell reference, text, or logical value.
lookup_array	Required. This is the list or range of cells to be searched.
match_type	Optional. This argument specifies how the function will behave. You have three options for this argument -1, 0, or 1. The default is 1 if the argument is omitted. **1 (or omitted)** = MATCH finds the largest value that is less than or equal to the lookup value. The values in the list must be in ascending order.

0 = MATCH finds the first value that's exactly equal to lookup_value. The values in the range can be in any order.

-1 = MATCH finds the smallest value that is greater than or equal to lookup_value. The values in the list must be in descending order.

Example 1

In the example below, we provide MATCH with a lookup_value of 21 (in cell B11), the lookup_array is B2:B9 and the match_type is set to 1.

=MATCH(B11, B2:B9, 1)

This means the function will return the row with the highest value that is *less than or equal to* 21. In this case, the value is 20 and the row is 5, so MATCH returns 5.

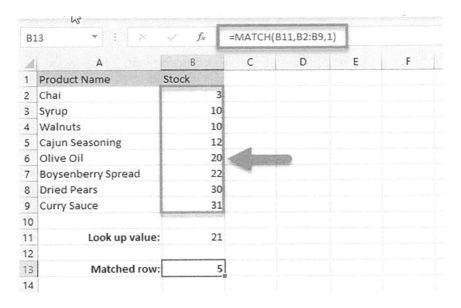

Example 2

	A	B	C	D	E
1	Product Name	Stock			
2	Curry Sauce	31			
3	Dried Pears	30			
4	Boysenberry Spread	22			
5	Olive Oil	20			
6	Cajun Seasoning	12			
7	Syrup	10			
8	Walnuts	10			
9	Chai	3			
10					
11	Look up value:	21			
12					
13	Matched row:	3			
14					

Cell B13 formula: =MATCH(B11,B2:B9,-1)

In this example, we provide the MATCH function with a lookup_value of **21**, the lookup_array is **B2:B9** and the match_type is set to **-1**.

=MATCH(B11, B2:B9, -1)

Result: 3

To use a match_type of -1, the range needs to be sorted in descending order. In this case, the function will return the row with the lowest value that is *greater than or equal to* 21. The value is 22 and the row is 3, so MATCH returns 3.

Example 3

If we use a match_type of 0 for both examples above, we'll get an error (#N/A) as MATCH will not be able to find an exact match in lookup_array.

If we use a lookup_value of 22 instead for the example:

=MATCH(22, B2:B9, 0)

MATCH will return 3 as 22 is in the third row of the range.

Product Name	Stock
Curry Sauce	31
Dried Pears	30
Boysenberry Spread	22
Olive Oil	20
Cajun Seasoning	12
Syrup	10
Walnuts	10
Chai	3

CHOOSE Function

The CHOOSE function allows you to use an index number to return a value from a list of arguments. You can use CHOOSE to select one out of a maximum of 254 values based on the index number.

Syntax

CHOOSE(index_num, value1, [value2], ...)

Arguments

Argument	Description
Index_num	Required. This argument specifies the value to be selected from the list. The Index_num argument must be a number between 1 and 254, or a formula, or cell reference that contains a number between 1 and 254.
Value1	Required. The first value is required. Values can be numbers, cell references, ranges, formulas, functions, or text.
[value2], ...	Optional. You can have up to 253 additional optional values.

Remarks

If the index_num argument is less than 1 or greater than the number of the last value in the list, CHOOSE returns an error (#VALUE!). If index_num is a fraction, it will be truncated to the lowest integer before it is used.

Example 1

Let's say we have the days of the week in a list and we want to return the day of the week for number 4.

=CHOOSE(4, Mon, Tue, Wed, Thu, Fri, Sat, Sun)

It will return "Thu", as this is the 4th item on the list.

Example 2

The CHOOSE function is most useful when used in combination with another function. For example, we can nest the CHOOSE function within the SUM function.

Let's say we want the SUM function to calculate a specific range on our worksheet from several ranges based on a number we provide. In the example below, we provide 4 to represent quarter four (QTR4) on the worksheet. The number is entered in cell B20.

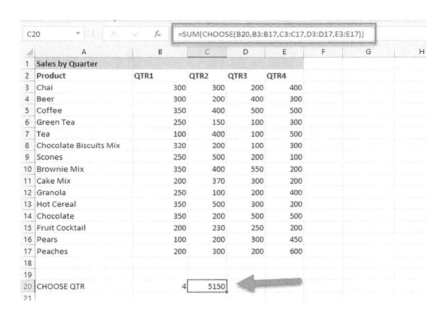

Formula explanation

The following formula is entered in cell C20:

=SUM(CHOOSE(B20,B3:B17,C3:C17,D3:D17,E3:E17))

Result: 5150

The CHOOSE function is first evaluated and it returns the range E3:E17. The SUM function then sums up E3:E17 to provide the total for that quarter.

Of course, looking at the example above, it may appear that it would be easier to just sum up each quarter separately. However, there may be situations when we want to do this, for example, as part of a summary report in another worksheet.

Tip: The CHOOSE function is useful for specific types of problems. For most lookup tasks in Excel, the VLOOKUP would suffice so I would recommend experimenting with VLOOKUP first to see if it would solve the problem before using CHOOSE.

TRANSPOSE Function

The TRANSPOSE function enables you to transpose data in your worksheet. If you want to rotate data on your worksheet you can use the Transpose option on the paste command. TRANSPOSE provides a way to carry out the same task without having to manually copy and paste the data. This can come in handy when you want to copy and transpose data from several ranges across different worksheets.

Syntax

TRANSPOSE(array)

Argument

The *Array* argument is required. This is a range of cells that you want to transpose.

Example:

In this example, we want to transpose the data in cells A1:B4 in the table below.

To get TRANSPOSE to work, ensure:

1. You select a destination range where the number of columns matches the number of rows in the source. For example, if the source has 4 rows then you must select 4 columns for the destination.
2. The number of rows in the destination should match the number of columns in the source.
3. You must also press CTRL+SHIFT+ENTER to enter the formula as it is an array function.

	A	B	C	D	E	F
1	QTR1	$2,000.00				
2	QTR2	$3,000.00				
3	QTR3	$1,400.00				
4	QTR4	$5,000.00				
5						
6						
7	QTR1	QTR2	QTR3	QTR4		
8	2000	3000	1400	5000		
9						
10						

Formula bar: A7 — {=TRANSPOSE(A1:B4)}

Steps to using TRANSPOSE:
1. Select the destination range.
2. In the formula bar, type **=TRANSPOSE(**
3. Enter the range, for example, A1:B4. You can manually enter this or select it on the worksheet by clicking and dragging from the beginning of the range to the end.
4. Type in the closing bracket but don't press Enter.
5. Press CTRL+SHIFT+ENTER

This will enclose the formula in curly brackets {}, indicating it is an array formula and the return values are across several cells.

ADDRESS function

You can use the ADDRESS function to return the address of a cell in a worksheet when you provide the row and column numbers as arguments. For example, =ADDRESS(4,6) returns $F$4.

Syntax

ADDRESS(row_num, column_num, [abs_num], [a1], [sheet_text])

Arguments

Argument	Description
row_num	Required. A number that specifies the row number to use in the cell reference.
column_num	Required. A number that specifies the column number to use in the cell reference.
abs_num	Optional. A number that specifies the type of reference to return, e.g. absolute, relative, or mixed references. The default is Absolute reference, and this will be used if abs_num is omitted. Argument values 1 (or omitted) = Absolute reference 2 = Mixed reference. Absolute row, relative column 3 = Mixed reference. Relative row, absolute column 4 = Relative reference
A1	Optional. This is a logical value that specifies whether to use the A1 or R1C1 style of reference. TRUE is A1 and FALSE is R1C1. If omitted, A1 is used.
sheet_text	Optional. This is a text value specifying the name of the worksheet to get the cell reference from. To be used when connecting to an external sheet. If this argument is omitted the current sheet is used.

Note: In Excel, A1 referencing means columns are labelled alphabetically and rows numerically. R1C1 referencing means both columns and rows are labelled numerically. The A1 reference style is the default and the recommendation for most occasions. However, if you need to change the reference style, click **File** > **Options** > **Formulas**. Under **Working with formulas**, check or uncheck the **R1C1 reference style** checkbox. The default reference style is A1 so R1C1 should be unchecked by default.

Examples

Example 1	
Formula:	=ADDRESS(2,4)
Description:	Absolute reference in the current sheet.
Result:	$D$2

Example 2	
Formula:	=ADDRESS(2,4,2)
Description:	Mixed reference. Absolute row; relative column.
Result:	D$2

Example 3	
Formula:	=ADDRESS(2,4,2,FALSE)
Description:	Mixed reference. Absolute row; relative column using the R1C1 reference style.
Result:	R2C[4]

Example 4	
Formula:	=ADDRESS(2,4,1,FALSE,"[Book2]Sheet1")
Description:	An absolute reference to another workbook (Book2) and worksheet.
Result:	[Book2]Sheet1!R2C4

Example 5	
Formula:	=ADDRESS(2,4,1,FALSE,"Accounts sheet")
Description:	An absolute reference to another worksheet.
Result:	'Accounts sheet'!R2C4

FORMULATEXT Function

The FORMULATEXT function enables you to display the formula from one cell in another cell in your worksheet. This is useful when you're trying to identify errors in your syntax or compare different formulas side by side. Instead of being able to only check your formulas one at a time by clicking on each cell, you can use the FORMULATEXT function to reveal the formulas in several cells at the same time.

Syntax

FORMULATEXT(reference)

Argument	Description
reference	Required. This can be a reference to a cell in the current workbook or another open workbook.

FORMULATEXT will return an #N/A error if:

- The cell used as the *Reference* argument does not contain a formula.
- *Reference* is in an external workbook that is not open.
- The formula can't be displayed due to worksheet protection.

If the Reference argument points to more than one cell, for example, a range, FORMULATEXT will return the value in the upper leftmost cell in the range.

Example

In this example, we have some values in column A. In column B we have several formulas used to aggregate the values from column A. To display the formulas on the sheet we use FORMULATEXT in column C.

	A	B	C
	Values	Aggregate results	Formula text
1			
2	$18.00	$126.35	=SUM(A2:A9)
3	$10.00	$21.06	=AVERAGE(A2:A9)
4	$22.00	6	=COUNT(A2:A9)
5	$21.35	$30.00	=MAX(A2:A9)
6	$25.00	$10.00	=MIN(A2:A9)
7	$30.00	$21.68	=MEDIAN(A2:A9)

C2: =FORMULATEXT(B2)

COLUMNS Function

The COLUMNS function returns the number of columns in an array or range. This function is mostly used as an argument in other functions. For example, in situations where you need to return the number of columns in a specified range as an argument of another function.

Syntax

COLUMNS(array)

Argument	Description
array	Required. This can be an array or a reference to a range of cells for which you want to count the number of columns.

Example

In this example, we want to count the number of columns in a dataset in cells A1:J5.

The formula used to get the count is:

=COLUMNS(A1:J5)

Result: 10.

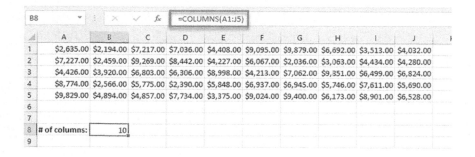

ROWS Function

The ROWS function returns the number of rows in an array or range. Like the COLUMNS function, the ROWS function is mostly useful as an argument within another function. For example, on occasions when you need to return the number of rows in a specified range as one of the arguments of another function.

Syntax

ROWS(array)

Argument	Description
array	Required. This can be an array or a reference to a range of cells for which you want to count the number of rows.

Example

In this example, we use ROWS to count the number of rows in a dataset in cells A1:E23.

Formula: =ROWS(A1:E23)

Result: 23

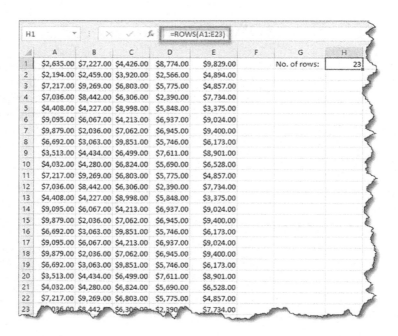

INDEX Function

The INDEX function enables you to return a value or a series of values from a range.

There are two forms of the INDEX function:
1. Array form
2. Reference form

INDEX Function - Array Form

The array form of this function can return a single value, an entire row, or an entire column from a chosen range.

Syntax

INDEX(array, [row_num], [column_num])

Arguments

Argument	Description
Array	Required. The *array* argument is a range of cells or an array constant. If the range contains only one row or column, the corresponding row_num or col_num is optional.
Row_num	If Row_num is omitted, Column_num is required. Selects the row in the *array* argument from which to return a value.
Column_num	If Column_num is omitted, Row_num is required. Selects the column in the *array* argument from which to return a value.

Remarks

- If the *array* argument has more than one row and more than one column, and only Row_num or Column_num is used, INDEX returns an array of the entire row or column in the *array* argument.

- INDEX returns a single value (at the intersection of Row_num and Column_num) if both arguments are used.

- INDEX returns an array of values, i.e. the entire column or row if you set Row_num or Column_num to 0 (zero).

- To return an entire row or column, you'll need to select the number of cells for the result (destination) that is equal to the number of cells of the source. For example, if the source *row* has 4 cells, you must select 4 cells horizontally for the result. Alternatively, if the source *column* has 4 cells, you must select 4 cells vertically for the result.

- You must press **CTRL+SHIFT+ENTER** to return the entire row or column. **Note**: If you just press enter, it will not work as expected.

Example 1

In this example, we return the value in Q3 for Toronto with the following formula:

=INDEX(B7:E10,3,4)

B7:E10 is the array, 3 is the row number, and 4 is the column number.

	A	B	C	D	E	F
1	Quaterly Data					
2					$6,306.00	
3						
4						
5			2015			
6		London	Paris	New York	Toronto	
7	Q1	$2,635.00	$2,194.00	$7,217.00	$7,036.00	
8	Q2	$7,227.00	$2,459.00	$9,269.00	$8,442.00	
9	Q3	$4,426.00	$3,920.00	$6,803.00	$6,306.00	
10	Q4	$8,774.00	$2,566.00	$5,775.00	$2,390.00	

Example 2

In this example, we can return the sum of the entire row for Q1 by combining the INDEX function with the SUM function.

We make the row_num argument 1 and the column_num argument 0 (zero), specifying that we want to return all the cells in row one from the range.

=SUM(INDEX(B7:E10,1,0))

	A	B	C	D	E	F
1	Quaterly Data					
2					$19,082.00	
3						
4						
5			2015			
6		London	Paris	New York	Toronto	
7	Q1	$2,635.00	$2,194.00	$7,217.00	$7,036.00	
8	Q2	$7,227.00	$2,459.00	$9,269.00	$8,442.00	
9	Q3	$4,426.00	$3,920.00	$6,803.00	$6,306.00	
10	Q4	$8,774.00	$2,566.00	$5,775.00	$2,390.00	

INDEX Function - Reference form

The reference form of the INDEX function returns the value of the cell at the intersection of a row and column. The reference argument can be made up of non-contiguous ranges and you can pick which range to search using the area_num argument.

Syntax

INDEX(reference,[row_num],[col_num],[area_num])

Arguments

Argument	Description
Reference	Required. A reference to one or more cell ranges. If you are entering more than one range for the reference, enclose this argument in parentheses. For example, INDEX((A1:B10,D1:D10),3,4)
Row_num	Required. Selects the row in the *array* argument from which to return a value. If Row_num is omitted, Column_num is required.
Column_num	Optional. Selects the column in the *array* argument from which to return a value. If Column_num is omitted, Row_num is required.
Area_num	Optional. Selects a range in *reference* from which the intersection of *Row_num* and *Column_num* will be returned. The first area is numbered 1, the second is 2, the third 3, and so on. If *Area_num* is left out of the formula, the default, area 1, will be used. The areas need to be on the same worksheet.

Remarks

- If you specify areas in *reference* that are not on the same worksheet as each other, the function will return an error (#VALUE!). If you need to use ranges that are on different worksheets, it's recommended that you use the array form of INDEX and use another function to generate the range that makes up the array. You could use the CHOOSE function, for example, to calculate which range will be used.

EXCEL 2019 FUNCTIONS

- If each area in reference contains only one row or column, the Row_num or Column_num argument, respectively, is optional. For example, for a single row reference, use INDEX(reference, column_num).

- Row_num and Column_num must point to a cell within *array* or the function will return an error (#REF!).

Example

In this example we have four ranges making up the *reference* argument:
1. 2015 = B7:E10
2. 2016 = H7:K10
3. 2017 = B14:E17
4. 2018 = H14:K17

To return a value from one of these ranges, we specify the range with *Area_num*. The ranges are numbered by the order of entry, starting from 1.

B7:E10 = 1; H7:K10 = 2; B14:E17 = 3; H14:K17 = 4

In this case, we've used a cell reference, J2, to enter the *Area_num* so that the value can be easily changed on the worksheet to point to a different range if needed.

=INDEX((B7:E10,H7:K10,B14:E17,H14:K17),3,4,J2)

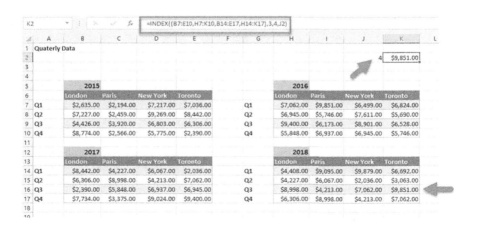

The formula returns **$9,851.00** from the third row and fourth column in the fourth range.

CHAPTER 3: LOGICAL FUNCTIONS

The logical functions in Excel can be found by clicking the Logical command button on the Formulas tab of the Ribbon. A logical function requires a logical test before carrying out one evaluation from several options. If the test evaluates to TRUE it executes one statement, and if the test is FALSE, it executes a different statement. A statement can be a calculation, a value, a string, or even another function. Logical functions can be nested, enabling you to carry out multiple logical tests before executing the statement.

In this chapter, we'll cover functions that enable you to:
- Select which statement to execute based on the result of a logical test.
- Check that multiple conditions are met with nested functions before executing a statement.
- Check that at least one of several conditions is met before executing a statement.
- Identify values in a list and provide replacement values.
- Trap errors in formulas and return a meaningful message.

IF Function

The IF function is one of the popular functions in Excel used to create conditional formulas. The IF function allows you to carry out a logical test (using comparison operators) that evaluates to TRUE or FALSE. The function executes one statement if the test is TRUE and another statement if the test is FALSE.

Syntax:

IF(logical_test, value_if_true, [value_if_false])

Arguments

Argument	Description
logical_test	Required. This is a value or expression that can be evaluated to TRUE or FALSE.
value_if_true	Required. This is the value that's returned if the logical test is true.
value_if_false	Optional. This is the value that's returned if the logical test is false. If the logical test is FALSE and this argument is omitted, nothing happens.

In its simplest form this is what the function says:

IF (something is TRUE, then do A, otherwise do B)

Therefore, the IF function will return a different result for TRUE and FALSE.

Example 1

A common way the IF function is used is to determine if a referenced cell has any value or not. If the result is 0 then it returns a blank cell.

In the example below, the formula for the total for ***Jan*** was entered in cell **I2** and we want to drag the formula down to populate the totals for ***Feb*** to ***Dec.*** Without the IF function, it would display $0 for the unpopulated months, however, we want the totals for the unpopulated months to be blank instead of $0 even with the formula in place.

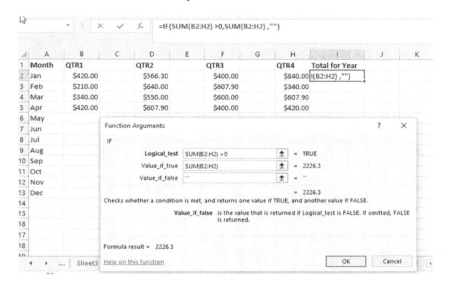

Thus, the formula for Jan in cell **I2** is:

=IF(SUM(B2:H2) >0,SUM(B2:H2) ,"")

The IF function in this example checks to see if the sum of Jan is greater than zero. If true it returns the sum. If it is false, then it returns a blank string.

When we populate the other fields with the formula, we get the following.

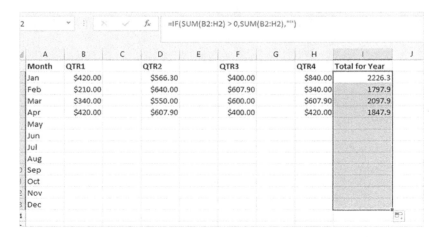

Example 2

In another example, we could use the results of an evaluation to return different values in our worksheet.

Let's say we have a budgeting sheet and want to use a "Status" column to report on how the **Actual** figure compares to the **Budgeted** figure. In this case, we can use the IF statement to test whether the actual figure is greater than the budgeted figure. If **Actual** is greater than **Budgeted**, the formula would enter "Over Budget", otherwise it would enter "Within Budget".

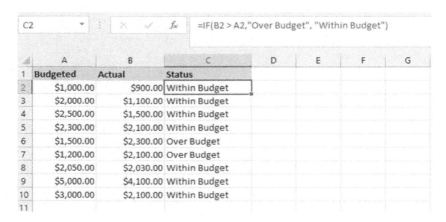

=IF(B2 > A2,"Over Budget", "Within Budget")

The IF function checks to see if the value in B2 is greater than the value in A2. If it is, it returns "Over Budget" otherwise it returns "Within Budget".

Example 3

In another example, say we have products for sale. When **10 or more** items are purchased, we apply a **10%** promotional discount.

	A	B	C	D	E
1	Product	Cost	Quantity	Sub-Total	Total (with discount)
2	Chai	$1.80	10	$18.00	$16.20
3	Beer	$1.50	15	$22.50	$20.25
4	Coffee	$2.00	25	$50.00	$45.00
5	Green Tea	$2.00	50	$100.00	$90.00
6	Tea	$1.30	20	$26.00	$23.40
7	Chocolate Biscuits Mix	$5.20	5	$26.00	$26.00
8	Scones	$4.90	5	$24.50	$24.50
9	Brownie Mix	$4.20	10	$42.00	$37.80
10	Cake Mix	$4.80	10	$48.00	$43.20
11					

Formula explanation

=IF(C2>=10,D2 - (D2 * 0.1),D2)

The logical test checks if C2 is greater than or equal to 10.

If true it returns the sub-total minus 10%.

If false it returns the sub-total.

The AutoFill handle was used to populate the other cells in the range E2:E10 with the formula.

Tip: The AutoFill handle appears as a plus sign (+) when you place the mouse pointer on the lower-right corner of the active cell.

Nested IF Functions

You can also use an IF function as an argument within an IF function. This is called a nested IF statement. You can nest up to seven IF statements. A nested IF statement might be required if you need to carry out more than one logical test in your function.

In the example below, we use a nested IF statement to test for 3 possible values and return a different result for each one.

We have a spreadsheet to record the score of exams and we want to mark everything under 40 as FAIL, between 40 and 69 as CREDIT, and 70 or more as MERIT.

The formula would look like this:

=IF(A2 < 40, "FAIL",IF(A2 < 70,"CREDIT","MERIT"))

	A	B
1	Score	Result
2	70	MERIT
3		

Formula explanation

=IF(A2 < 40, "FAIL",IF(A2 < 70,"CREDIT","MERIT"))

The first IF statement checks if A2 is less than 40. If it is TRUE, it returns "FAIL" and ends the evaluation there. If A2 < 40 is FALSE, the second IF test is executed.

The second IF function checks if A2 is less than 70. If true it returns "CREDIT", and if false, it returns "MERIT".

Tip: The IFS function was introduced in Excel 2016 as a better way of addressing multiple logical tests in one formula. As much as possible, use IFS in place of multiple nested IF statements. It is much easier to read when you have multiple tests.

Advanced IF Functions

An advanced IF function is a hybrid of a logical function and a statistics or mathematics function. Advanced IF functions are covered in more detail in this book in the chapters for Maths Functions and Statistical Functions. In this section, we briefly examine some of the important advanced IF functions you can use as one solution instead of combining two functions.

AVERAGEIF

Syntax:

=AVERAGEIF(range, criteria, [average_range])

This function returns the average (arithmetic mean) of data that meets the value you've entered as criteria. The optional *average_range* argument allows you to specify another range for the values if it is separate from the one with the criteria.

Example:

=AVERAGEIF(A2:A20,"<2000")

This means, return the average of all the values in cells A2 to A20 that are greater than 2000.

AVERAGEIFS

Syntax:

=AVERAGEIFS(average_range, criteria_range1, criteria1, [criteria_range2, criteria2], ...)

This function is similar to AVERAGEIF, however, it allows you to specify multiple ranges and multiple criteria in the arguments. You can specify up to 127 ranges and criteria.

COUNTIF

This function returns the count of the values in a range that meets the specified criteria.

Syntax:

=COUNTIF(range, criteria)

In its simplest form this function says:

=COUNTIF(Where do you want to look?, What do you want to look for?)

Example:

=COUNTIF(A2:A10,"New York")

This will return the count of the number of cells in A2:A10 with the value "New York".

COUNTIFS

COUNTIFS(criteria_range1, criteria1, [criteria_range2, criteria2]…)

This function is like the COUNTIF function in that it returns a count based on a condition you specify. However, you can specify multiple ranges and criteria. You can specify up to 127 range/criteria pairs.

SUMIF

This function returns the sum of values in a range that match a given criterion.

Example:

=SUMIF(A2:A10, ">10")

This means, return the sum of all the values in cells A2 to A10 that are greater than 10.

SUMIFS

Syntax:

SUMIFS(sum_range, criteria_range1, criteria1, [criteria_range2, criteria2], ...)

This function returns the sum of values that meet several criteria. You can specify up to 127 range/criteria pairs.

Note: All advanced IF functions briefly touched on above are covered in more detail elsewhere in this book. Check the table of contents for which chapter a function has been covered.

IFS Function

The IFS function enables you to carry out multiple logical tests and execute a statement that corresponds to the first test that is TRUE. The tests need to be entered in the order in which you want the statements executed so that the right result is returned as soon as a test is passed. IFS was created as a better approach to nested IF statements which can quickly become too complex.

Note: The IFS function was introduced in Excel 2016. If you're subscribed to Office 365, ensure you have the latest version of Office installed.

Syntax

IFS(logical_test1, value_if_true1, [logical_test2, value_if_true2], [logical_test3, value_if_true3],...)

Arguments

Argument	Description
logical_test1	Required. This is the condition that is being tested. It can evaluate to TRUE or FALSE.
value_if_true1	Required. The result to be returned if logical_test1 evaluates to TRUE.
logical_test2... logical_test127	Optional. A condition that evaluates to TRUE or FALSE. You can have up to 127 tests in total.
value_if_true2... value_if_true127	Optional. The results to be returned if logical_test2...logical_test127 evaluates to TRUE.

Remarks

The IFS function allows you to test up to 127 different tests. However, it is generally advised not to use too many tests with IF or IFS statements. This is because multiple tests need to be entered in the right order and it can become too complex to update or maintain.

Tip: As much as possible, use IFS in place of multiple nested IF statements. It is much easier to read when you have multiple conditions.

Example 1

In the example below, we use the IFS function to solve a problem we addressed earlier with nested IF statements.

In this problem, we want to assign grades to different ranges of exam scores.

<u>Score and Grades</u>
1. 70 or above = MERIT
2. 50 to 69 = CREDIT
3. 40 to 49 = PASS
4. less than 40 = FAIL

We derive the following formula to achieve our aim:

=IFS(A2>=70,"MERIT",A2>=50,"CREDIT", A2>=40,"PASS", A2<40,"FAIL")

	A	B
1	Score	Grade
2	70	MERIT
3	60	CREDIT
4	35	FAIL
5	40	PASS
6	85	MERIT
7	60	CREDIT

Formula explanation

=IFS(A2>=70,"MERIT",A2>=50,"CREDIT", A2>=40,"PASS", A2<40,"FAIL")

The IFS function as been used to create four logical tests in sequential order:

A2>=70,"MERIT"
A2>=50,"CREDIT"
A2>=40,"PASS"
A2<40,"FAIL"

A2 is a reference to the score. As you can see, each score is tested against each condition in sequential order. As soon as a test is passed the corresponding grade is returned and no further testing is carried out.

Example 2

In this example, we want to set different priority levels for reordering items depending on the number of items in stock.

Priority Level:
1. 5 or less = 1
2. 10 or less = 2
3. Less than 20 = 3

The formula we use to accomplish this task is:

=IFS(A2>20,"N/A",A2<=5,1, A2<=10,2, A2<20,3)

	A	B
1	In stock	Priority Level
2	10	2
3	25	N/A
4	9	2
5	10	2
6	4	1
7	10	2
8	15	3
9	10	2
10	10	2
11	5	1
12	10	2
13	5	1
14	15	3

Formula explanation

=IFS(A2>20,"N/A",A2<=5,1, A2<=10,2, A2<20,3)

First, we insert a test to mark the Priority Level for any products greater than 20 as "N/A" (not applicable) as those have no re-order priority yet. Then we carry out the tests in sequential order from the smallest value to the largest to ensure that the right corresponding value is returned as soon as a test is passed.

You can also apply conditional formatting to the results column to highlight the records with the highest priority. In this case, 1 is the highest priority.

Tip: For instructions on how to apply conditional formatting to cells, see my book *Excel 2019 Basics*.

SWITCH Function

The SWITCH function evaluates an expression against a list of values and returns the value that corresponds to the first match. If no match is found, an optional default value may be returned.

Note: The SWITCH function was introduced in Excel 2016 so will not be available in an earlier version of Excel. If you're subscribed to Office 365, ensure that you have the latest version of Office.

Syntax

SWITCH(expression, value1, result1, [default or value2, result2],…[default or value3, result3])

Arguments

Argument	Description
expression	Required. The expression argument is the value that will be compared against the list of values in value1…value126. *Expression* can be a number, date or some text.
value1…value126	The value argument is a value that will be compared with the expression argument. You can have up to 126 values.
result1…result126	This is the value to be returned when the corresponding argument matches the *expression* argument. A *result* must be supplied for each corresponding *value* argument. You can have up to 126 results to match each value argument.
default	Optional. Default is the value to be returned if no match is found. *Default* must be the last argument in the function, and it is identified by not having a corresponding result value.

Excel functions are limited to 254 arguments, so you can only use up to 126 pairs of *value* and *result* arguments.

Example

In the following example, we have a column of numbers and we would like to switch the numbers to text descriptions that describe the numbers in a more meaningful way.

List of values we want to switch:
    1 = Quarter 1
    2 = Quarter 2
    3 = Quarter 3
    3 = Quarter 4

Formula:

=SWITCH(A2,1,"Quarter 1",2,"Quarter 2",3,"Quarter 3",4,"Quarter 4","No match")

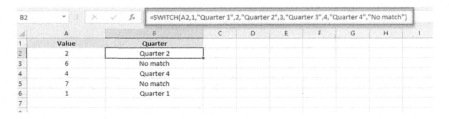

On the occasions when no match is found like in 6 and 7, the default value, "No Match", is returned.

Tip: The *result* arguments have been entered directly in the formula here for demonstration purposes only. In a production worksheet, it would be better to enter the values in a lookup range in your worksheet and then use cell references in your formula. That way it is easier to maintain.

IFERROR Function

This function is used to trap errors in Excel formulas and return a meaningful message. It is like how errors are trapped and handled in computer code. IFERROR can trap the following error types: #VALUE!, #N/A, #DIV/0!, #REF!, #NAME?, #NUM!, or #NULL!.

Syntax

IFERROR(value, value_if_error)

Arguments

Argument	Description
Value	Required. This is the argument that is checked for an error. This can be a cell reference or a formula.
Value_if_error	Required. This is the value that is returned if the formula evaluates to an error.

Remarks

- If either *value* or *value_if_error* points to an empty cell, IFERROR treats it as an empty string value ("").

- If *value* is an array formula, IFERROR returns an array of results, one for each cell in the results range.

Example

In the following example, we use the IFERROR formula to trap any errors in our formula in column C and return a text message "Calculation error".

For the purpose of this exercise, the FORMULATEXT function has been used in D2:D5 to reveal the formulas in columns C2:C5.

C2	:	× ✓ fx	=IFERROR(B2/A2,"Calculation error")	
	A	B	C	D
1	Target	Actual Units Sold	Percentage	
2	200	35	18%	=IFERROR(B2/A2,"Calculation error")
3	10	0	0%	=IFERROR(B3/A3,"Calculation error")
4	120	50	42%	=IFERROR(B4/A4,"Calculation error")
5		5	Calculation error	=IFERROR(B5/A5,"Calculation error")

AND Function

The AND function is used to determine if all conditions in a test are TRUE. This is useful for problems where you want to carry out more than one logical test and you want to check that they all evaluate to TRUE. This function is useful for situations where you want to check that several prerequisites are met before a condition is applied.

Syntax

AND(logical1, [logical2], ...)

Arguments

Argument	Description
Logical1	Required. This is the first condition that you want to test that can either evaluate to TRUE or FALSE.
Logical2, ...	Optional. You can have up to 254 additional conditions you want to test that can evaluate to either TRUE or FALSE.

Remarks

- The arguments must evaluate to logical values (i.e. TRUE or FALSE) or must be references to cells that contain logical values.

- If an argument contains an array or reference that points to text or empty cells, those values will be ignored.

- If the specified range contains no logical values, the #VALUE! error is returned by the AND function.

Example

In this example, we want to apply a discount for order items that meet a certain criterion.

We want a formula that:
1. Checks that a product is on promotion.
2. Checks that the number of units ordered is 3 or more.

3. Apply a discount if the item is on promotion and 3 or more have been ordered.

	A	B	C
1	Product Name	On Promotion	Units Ordered
2	Chai	Yes	3
3	Syrup	Yes	1
4	Cajun Seasoning	Yes	6
5	Olive Oil	No	7
6	Boysenberry Spread	Yes	1
7	Dried Pears	No	1
8	Curry Sauce	Yes	2
9	Walnuts	Yes	3
10	Fruit Cocktail	No	4
11	Chocolate Biscuits Mix	Yes	2
12	Marmalade	Yes	3
13	Scones	Yes	5
14	Beer	Yes	10
15	Crab Meat	No	7

The AND formula we use to carry out both tests is:

AND(B2="yes",C2>=3)

Next, we use the AND function as an argument inside an IF function. The IF statement returns "Apply discount" if our AND statement returns TRUE, and "No discount" if our AND statement returns FALSE.

The final formula looks like this:

=IF(AND(B2="yes",C2>=3)=TRUE,"Apply discount","No discount")

	A	B	C	D	E	F
1	Product Name	On Promotion	Units Ordered	Discount status		
2	Chai	Yes	3	Apply discount		
3	Syrup	Yes	1	No discount		
4	Cajun Seasoning	Yes	6	Apply discount		
5	Olive Oil	No	7	No discount		
6	Boysenberry Spread	Yes	1	No discount		
7	Dried Pears	No	1	No discount		
8	Curry Sauce	Yes	2	No discount		
9	Walnuts	Yes	3	Apply discount		
10	Fruit Cocktail	No	4	No discount		
11	Chocolate Biscuits Mix	Yes	2	No discount		
12	Marmalade	Yes	3	Apply discount		
13	Scones	Yes	5	Apply discount		
14	Beer	Yes	10	Apply discount		
15	Crab Meat	No	7	No discount		
16						

D2 ▼ : × ✓ *fx* =IF(AND(B2="yes",C2>=3)=TRUE,"Apply discount","No discount")

The AND function has been combined with the IF function to make it more robust. Using AND as an argument in IF enabled us to carry out two logical tests within its *logical_test* argument and return one logical value.

OR Function

The OR function is used to determine if any conditions in a test are TRUE. This is useful for problems where you want to carry out more than one logical test and you want to return a value if at least one of them evaluates to TRUE.

This function is best used in conjunction with other logical functions for more complex test scenarios involving multiple logical tests. For example, the IF function requires you to test a condition to determine which return statement to execute. If you combine IF and OR, it enables you to test multiple conditions instead of just one.

Syntax

OR(logical1, [logical2], ...)

Arguments

Argument	Description
Logical1	Required. This is the first condition that you want to test that can either evaluate to TRUE or FALSE.
Logical2, ...	Optional. You can have up to 254 additional conditions you want to test that can evaluate to either TRUE or FALSE.

Remarks

- The maximum number of arguments you can have for the OR functions is 255.

- The arguments must evaluate to logical values (i.e. TRUE or FALSE) or must be references to cells that contain logical values.

- If an argument contains references that point to text or empty cells, those values will be ignored.

- If the specified range contains no logical values, the #VALUE! error is returned by the AND function.

EXCEL 2019 FUNCTIONS

Example

In this example, we need to determine which sales staff qualify for a sales commission based on the sales they've generated.

The sales figures are in the table below. Under the main table, we have a lookup table for the Amount per Criteria. These are the goals to be referenced in our formula to calculate the **Commission** for each salesperson.

The IF function can be used in combination with OR to achieve our aim.

The following formula is entered in cell D2 and copied down to the other cells in column D using the Fill Handle.

=IF(OR(B2>=$B$15,C2>=$B$16),B2*$B$17,0)

	A	B	C	D	E
1	Name	Sales	Signups	Commission	Bonus
2	Nancy Freehafer	$12,500	20	$250	$188
3	Andrew Cencini	$14,300	25	$286	$215
4	Jan Kotas	$9,000	10	$180	$0
5	Mariya Sergienko	$8,050	5	$161	$0
6	Steven Thorpe	$5,000	7	$0	$0
7	Michael Neipper	$8,900	10	$178	$0
8	Robert Zare	$7,900	10	$0	$0
9	Laura Giussani	$6,000	17	$120	$0
10	Anne Hellung-Larsen	$11,000	18	$220	$0
11					
12					
13					
14	Criteria	Amount			
15	Sales Goal	$8,000			
16	Signup Goal	15			
17	Commission	2.0%			
18	Bonus Goal	$12,000			
19	Bonus %	1.5%			

- Sales people need to exceed Sales Goal OR Signup Goal to earn a **Commission**.

- Sales people need to exceed Sales Goal AND Signup Goal to earn a **Bonus**.

Formula explanation

=IF(OR(B2>=$B$15,C2>=$B$16),B2*$B$17,0)

The formula says:

IF **Sales** are greater than or equal to (>=) the **Sales Goal**, OR **Signups** are greater than or equal to (>=) the **Signup Goal**, then multiply Sales by the Commission (2.0%), otherwise, return 0.

CHAPTER 4: MATH FUNCTIONS

The mathematics functions in Excel can be found by clicking the Math & Trig command button on the Formulas tab of the Ribbon. The drop-down menu lists all the Math & Trig functions. This category of functions in Excel ranges from common arithmetic functions to complex functions used by mathematicians and engineers.

Our focus here will be on the arithmetic functions as many of the trigonometric functions are applicable to mathematics problems requiring specialist knowledge that's outside the scope of this book.

In this chapter, we'll cover functions that enable you to:
- Sum up data in contiguous or non-contiguous ranges.
- Sum up data based on certain criteria using a single function.
- Use multiple criteria to determine which data to add up.
- Automatically generate random numbers between two given numbers.
- Automatically round up or round down numbers with a function.
- Calculate the square root of a number.

SUM Function

The SUM function enables you to add values on your spreadsheet. You can add individual values, cell references, ranges or a mix of all three. You can sum up contiguous cells or non-contiguous cells.

Syntax

SUM(number1,[number2],...)

Arguments

Argument	Description
Number1	Required. The first cell reference, range, or number for which you want to calculate the sum. The argument can be a number like 4, a cell reference like A10, or a range like A2:A10.
Number2, ...	Optional. Additional cell references, ranges or numbers for which you want to calculate the sum, up to a maximum of 255.

Example 1

In this example, we have values in cells B2 to B13 that you want to sum up.

We could either use the AutoSum command on the ribbon or enter the formula in the formula bar:

=SUM(B2:B13)

EXCEL 2019 FUNCTIONS

	A	B	C	D	E
	SUM	▾ : × ✓ fx	=SUM(B2:B13)		
1	Month	Expenses			
2	Jan	$400.00			
3	Feb	$640.00			
4	Mar	$550.00			
5	Apr	$420.00			
6	May	$310.50			
7	Jun	$566.30			
8	Jul	$607.90			
9	Aug	$300.80			
10	Sep	$500.50			
11	Oct	$700.00			
12	Nov	$840.00			
13	Dec	$900.00			
14	Sum	=SUM(B2:B13)			
15		SUM(**number1**, [number2], ...)			
16					

Example 2

To sum up data in different ranges, i.e. non-contiguous data, you can enter the ranges as different arguments in the SUM function.

=SUM(B2:B13,D2:D13,F2:F13,H2:H13)

	A	B	C	D	E	F	G	H	I
1	Month	Year 1		Year 2		Year 3		Year 4	
2	Jan	$420.00		$566.30		$400.00		$840.00	
3	Feb	$210.00		$640.00		$607.90		$340.00	
4	Mar	$340.00		$550.00		$600.00		$607.90	
5	Apr	$420.00		$607.90		$400.00		$420.00	
6	May	$310.50		$500.00		$210.00		$400.00	
7	Jun	$500.00		$566.30		$420.00		$607.90	
8	Jul	$300.00		$607.90		$505.00		$790.00	
9	Aug	$700.00		$400.00		$500.00		$733.00	
10	Sep	$410.00		$500.50		$900.00		$500.50	
11	Oct	$800.00		$607.90		$700.00		$600.00	
12	Nov	$840.00		$840.00		$840.00		$300.00	
13	Dec	$900.00		$1,100.00		$1,200.00		$1,000.00	
14									
15	Total							3,H2:H13)	

SUMIF Function

The SUMIF function is the combination of a math function and a logical function. It allows you to sum up data in a range of cells based on a certain criterion.

Syntax

SUMIF(range, criteria, [sum_range])

Arguments

Argument	Description
range	Required. This is the range of cells that you want to evaluate based on the condition in *criteria*.
criteria	Required. This is the condition (or logical test) that is used to determine which cells are summed up in *range*. This can be an expression, cell reference, text, or function. **Note:** If this argument is text or includes logical or mathematical symbols like greater than (>), for example, it must be enclosed in double-quotes (""). If *criteria* is numeric, quotation marks are not required.
sum_range	Optional. You use this argument if you want to add up values in a different range from those specified in the range argument. If this argument is omitted, then the cells specified in *range* are used.

Remarks

- Cells in the range argument must be numbers, names (for example, named ranges or tables), arrays, or references that contain numbers. Text values and blanks are ignored.

- You can use wildcard characters (like a question mark "?" or an asterisk "*") as the criteria argument. A question mark matches any single character while an asterisk matches any sequence of characters.

Type a tilde (~) before the character if you want to find an actual question mark or asterisk.

Example 1

In this example, we're using SUMIF to sum up all Sales over $5,000.

The formula used is:

=SUMIF(A2:A11,">5000")

	A	B	C	D
1	Sales	Commission		
2	$2,635	$132		
3	$7,227	$361		
4	$4,426	$221		
5	$4,774	$239		
6	$9,829	$491		
7	$20,000	$1,000		
8	$2,459	$123		
9	$11,300	$565		
10	$2,566	$128		
11	$10,894	$545		
12				
13	Report			
14	$59,250		Sum of sales over $5,000	
15	$2,963		Commission for sales over $5,000	
16				

The formula is using the criteria argument of ">5000" to filter which values will be added to the sum from the range A2:A11.

Example 2

In this example, we're using SUMIF to sum up all Commissions for sales over $5,000. We'll be using the *sum_range* argument to specify the cells we want to sum up as they are different from the cells specified in the *range* argument.

The formula we use is:

=SUMIF(A2:A11,">5000", B2:B11)

	A	B	C	D
1	Sales	Commission		
2	$2,635	$132		
3	$7,227	$361		
4	$4,426	$221		
5	$4,774	$239		
6	$9,829	$491		
7	$20,000	$1,000		
8	$2,459	$123		
9	$11,300	$565		
10	$2,566	$128		
11	$10,894	$545		
12				
13	Report			
14	$59,250		Sum of sales over $5,000	
15	$2,963		Commission for sales over $5,000	
16				
17				

(Cell A15 shown in formula bar: =SUMIF(A2:A11,">5000", B2:B11))

Formula explanation

=SUMIF(A2:A11,">5000", B2:B11)

The formula is using the criteria argument ">5000" to select the values in column A (Sales) for which the corresponding values in column B (Commission) will be added to the sum. So, even though we applied the criteria to column A, the values summed up come from Column B.

SUMIFS Function

The SUMIFS function is like the SUMIF function however you can use multiple criteria to determine which cells in a range are included in the sum. SUMIFS enables you to have up to a total of 127 range/criteria pairs.

Syntax

SUMIFS(sum_range, criteria_range1, criteria1, [criteria_range2, criteria2], ...)

Arguments

Argument	Description
Sum_range	Required. This is the range of cells you want to sum up.
Criteria_range1	Required. The range that is tested using *Criteria1*. *Criteria_range1* and *Criteria1* are a pair where *Criteria1* is used to search *Criteria_range1* for matching values. Once items in the range are found, their corresponding values in *Sum_range* are added.
Criteria1	Required. This is the criteria used to apply the filter on criteria1_range that selects the data subset. For example, criteria can be entered as 40, ">40", C6, "bolts", or "125".
Criteria_range2, criteria2, ...	Optional. You can have additional range/criteria pairs up to a maximum of 127 pairs in total.

Remarks

- If you are testing for text values, make sure the criterion is in quotation marks.

- You can use wildcard characters like the question mark (?) and asterisk (*) in your criteria to enable you to find matches that are not exact but similar. The question mark matches any single character and the asterisk matches a sequence of characters. To find a character like a question mark or asterisk, type a tilde sign (~) in front of the character.

- The *Criteria_range* argument must reference a range that has the same number of rows and columns as the *Sum_range* argument.

Example

In the following example, we want to sum up Sales totals using 2 criteria.
1. State name
2. Orders that are greater than or equal to 40 (>=40)

Formula

=SUMIFS($D$2:$D$12,$B$2:$B$12,F2,$C$2:$C$12,G2)

	A	B	C	D	E	F	G	H
1	Name	States	No. Orders	Sales		States	Orders	Total Sales for matching orders
2	Bruce	New York	51	$74,298		New York	>=40	$140,407
3	Louis	New York	39	$46,039		Texas	>=40	$44,390
4	Earl	Washington	60	$65,252		California	>=40	$42,484
5	Sean	Washington	100	$61,847		Washington	>=40	$127,099
6	Benjamin	Texas	28	$33,340				
7	Joe	California	31	$95,778				
8	Shawn	Texas	35	$58,808				
9	Kenneth	California	39	$52,593				
10	Cynthia	California	51	$42,484				
11	Susan	Texas	80	$44,390				
12	Dav	New York	70	$66,109				

Formula explanation

=SUMIFS($D$2:$D$12,$B$2:$B$12,F2,$C$2:$C$12,G2)

- The *Sum_range* argument references the Sales column **D2:D12** (an absolute reference has been used - **$D$2:$D$12**).

    Tip: To convert *Sum_range* to an absolute reference, you can add the dollar signs manually in the formula bar or click on the reference within the formula (i.e. D2:D12) and press the F4 key. This ensures that the reference will not change when the formula is copied to other cells.

- The *Criteria_range1* is **B2:B12** (an absolute reference has also been used here - **$B$2:$B$12**)

Press F4, with the argument selected, to make this an absolute reference.

- The *Criteria1* argument is **F2**. This is a reference to the States we want to use as our criteria. A cell reference has been used for this argument to make it easier to change. This has been left as a relative reference because we want it to change relatively as we copy the formula to other cells.

- The *Criteria_range2* is **$C$2:$C$12** (in absolute reference form).

- The *Criteria2* argument is **G2** (>=40). A cell reference has been used for this argument to make it easier to change.

We enter the formula in cell **H2** and then copy it down the column to sum up the **Total Sales** for orders that match the criteria for each state.

AGGREGATE Function

The AGGREGATE function returns an aggregate in a list or database. This function brings together all the aggregate functions into one. Instead of using individual aggregate functions, like SUM, AVG, MAX etc. you simply enter a number in one of its arguments to specify the type of aggregate you want to execute. You can also set the option to ignore hidden rows and error values.

There are two forms of the AGGREGATE function:
1. Reference form
2. Array form

Syntax

Reference form

AGGREGATE(function_num, options, ref1, [ref2], ...)

Array form

AGGREGATE(function_num, options, array, [k])

Arguments

Function_num: Required. The *function_num* argument is a number between 1 to 19. This is the number that specifies which aggregate function to use. See the list below.

1=AVERAGE	2=COUNT	3=COUNTA
4=MAX	5=MIN	6=PRODUCT
7=STDEV.S	8=STDEV.P	9=SUM
10=VAR.S	11=VAR.P	12=MEDIAN
13=MODE.SNGL	14=LARGE	15=SMALL
16=PERCENTILE.INC	17=QUARTILE.INC	18=PERCENTILE.EXC
19=QUARTILE.EXC		

Options: Required. This argument is a numerical value from 1 to 7 that determines which values to ignore in the range we want to evaluate.

Options and behaviour:

- 0 or omitted=Ignore nested AGGREGATE and SUBTOTAL functions
- 1=Ignore hidden rows, nested AGGREGATE and SUBTOTAL functions
- 2=Ignore error values, nested AGGREGATE and SUBTOTAL functions
- 3=Ignore hidden rows, error values, nested AGGREGATE and SUBTOTAL functions
- 4=Ignore nothing
- 5=Ignore hidden rows
- 6=Ignore error values
- 7=Ignore hidden rows and error values

Ref1: Required. This is the first numeric argument for functions that take multiple numeric arguments for ranges that you want to aggregate. Ref1 can be a range, an array (for functions that take an array), or a formula.

Ref2,... Optional. This is for additional numeric arguments. You can have up to 253 arguments in total for which you want the aggregate value.

For the functions that take an array argument, ref1 will be an array, an array formula, or a reference to the range we want to aggregate. Ref2 is a second argument that is required for some functions. The functions listed below require a ref2 argument:

- LARGE(array,k)
- SMALL(array,k)
- PERCENTILE.INC(array,k)
- QUARTILE.INC(array,quart)
- PERCENTILE.EXC(array,k)

- QUARTILE.EXC(array,quart)

Remarks

- As soon as you type **=AGGREGATE(** in the formula bar you'll see a drop-down list of all functions that you can use as arguments for *function_num*. For the *options* argument, you'll also get a dropdown list for the values you can enter.

- AGGREGATE will return a #VALUE! error if a second ref argument is required but not provided.

- The AGGREGATE function is designed for columns of data i.e. ranges that are vertical. It is not designed for rows of data i.e. ranges that are horizontal.

Examples

In the following example, we'll use different instances of the AGGREGATE function to evaluate the data in the range below.

	A	B	C
1	#DIV/0!	56	
2	90	81	
3	31	95	
4	#NUM!	49	
5	41	34	
6	150	92	
7	34	58	
8	87	93	
9	33	120	
10	53	89	
11	74	92	
12			
13			

Example 1 - MAX	
Formula	=AGGREGATE(4, 6, A1:A11)
Result	150
Description	Returns the maximum value in range A1:A11 while ignoring error values in the range.

Example 2 - LARGE	
Formula	=AGGREGATE(14, 6, A1:A11, 3)
Result	87
Description	Returns the third largest value in range A1:A11 while ignoring error values in the range.

Example 3 - SMALL	
Formula	=AGGREGATE(15, 6, A1:A11)
Result	#VALUE!
Description	Returns a #VALUE! error because AGGREGATE is expecting a second ref argument here. The function referenced (SMALL) requires one.

Example 4 - MEDIAN	
Formula	=AGGREGATE(12, 6, A1:A11, B1:B11)
Result	77.5
Description	Returns the median from both columns while ignoring error values in the range.

Example 5	
Formula	=MAX(A1:A2)
Result	#DIV/0!
Description	Returns an error value since there are error values in the referenced range.

Tip: The AGGREGATE function will be overkill for the common aggregate tasks in Excel like sum, average, count etc. Only use this function if you're calculating one of the more complex aggregate types like STDEV.S, QUARTILE.INC, PERCENTILE.INC etc. For everyday aggregate tasks, use the standard functions like SUM, AVG, MIN and MAX.

MOD Function

The MOD function is useful for calculations where you want to return the remainder of a division between two numbers. The result has the same sign as the divisor.

Syntax

MOD(number, divisor)

Arguments

Argument	Description
Number	Required. The number being divided for which you want to find the remainder.
Divisor	Required. The number being used for the division. MOD will return the #DIV/0! error value if the divisor is 0.

Example

Formula	Result	Description
=MOD(4, 3)	1	Reminder 4/3
=MOD(-4, 3)	1	Reminder -4/3 **Note**: MOD returns a result with the same sign as the divisor.
=MOD(4, -3)	-1	Reminder 4/-3
=MOD(-4, -3)	-1	Reminder -4/-3

RANDBETWEEN Function

The RANDBETWEEN function returns a random integer between two numbers you specify. This function comes in handy when you want to generate sample data between two numbers. For example, if you want to generate some sample data between 1 and 100 in several cells, you could use RANDBETWEEN to generate a random number in one cell and copy the formula over the required range.

Syntax

RANDBETWEEN(bottom, top)

Arguments

Argument	Description
Bottom	Required. The smallest integer to be returned.
Top	Required. The largest integer to be returned.

The random values are regenerated each time the worksheet is recalculated. Hence, if you generate random values that you don't want to change each time the worksheet is recalculated, you need to copy only the values to another range without the formulas.

Example

In this example, we will use the RANDBETWEEN function to generate sample data for student scores between 0 and 100.

	A	B	C	D	E	F
				=RANDBETWEEN(0,100)		
1	Test Score Sample Data					
2						
3	Student	Score				
4	Bruce	64				
5	Louis	90				
6	Earl	56				
7	Sean	61				
8	Benjamin	46				
9	Joe	49				
10	Shawn	78				
11	Kenneth	33				
12	Cynthia	85				
13	Susan	55				
14						
15						

(Cell reference: B4)

Tip: To keep only the generated values without the formula, generate the sample data in a different part of your worksheet and then copy and paste only the values into your target range. For example, if you wanted random values in cells B2:B10, generate the values using RANDBETWEEN in cells F2:F10 and then copy and paste only the values in B2:B10, then delete the values in F2:F10.

ROUND Function

The ROUND function rounds a number to a specified number of digits. For example, if you have 25.4568 in cell A1 and you want to round the figure to two decimal places, you can use the following formula:

=ROUND(A1, 2)

The function will return: 25.46

Syntax

ROUND(number, num_digits)

Arguments

Argument	Description
number	Required. This argument is the number that you want to round.
num_digits	Required. This is the number of decimal places to which you want to round the number.

Remarks

- The number is rounded to the specified number of decimal places if num_digits is greater than 0 (zero).

- The number is rounded to the nearest integer if num_digits is 0.

- The number is rounded to the left of the decimal point if num_digits is less than 0.

- Use the ROUNDUP function if you want to always round up (away from zero).

- Use the ROUNDDOWN function if you want to always round down (toward zero).

Examples

In the following examples, the ROUND function is applied to several values. The table displays the formula, the result, and a description of the outcome.

Formula	Result	Description
=ROUND(3.15, 1)	3.2	Rounds 3.15 to one decimal place.
=ROUND(4.149, 1)	4.1	Rounds 4.149 to one decimal place.
=ROUND(-2.475, 2)	-2.48	Rounds -2.475 to two decimal places.
=ROUND(57.5, -1)	60	Rounds 57.5 to one decimal place to the left of the decimal point.
=ROUND(671.3,-3)	1000	Rounds 671.3 to the nearest multiple of 1000.
=ROUND(1.78,-1)	0	Rounds 1.78 to the nearest multiple of 10.
=ROUND(-70.45,-2)	-100	Rounds -70.45 to the nearest multiple of 100.

ROUNDUP Function

The ROUNDUP function rounds a number up, away from 0 (zero).

Syntax

ROUNDUP(number, num_digits)

Arguments

Argument	Description
Number	Required. This argument is for the number that you want to round up.
Num_digits	Required. The number of decimal places to which you want to round up the number.

Remarks

- ROUNDUP is like ROUND, except that it always rounds a number up.

- *Number* is rounded up to the specified number of decimal places if num_digits is greater than 0 (zero).

- *Number* is rounded up to the nearest integer if num_digits is 0.

- *Number* is rounded up to the left of the decimal point if num_digits is less than 0.

Examples

In the following examples, ROUNDUP is applied to several values. The table displays the formula, the result, and a description of the outcome.

Formula	Result	Description
=ROUNDUP(3.15, 1)	3.2	Rounds 3.15 up to one decimal place.
=ROUNDUP(4.149, 1)	5	Rounds 4.149 up to zero decimal places.
=ROUNDUP(-2.475, 2)	-2.48	Rounds -2.475 to two decimal places.
=ROUNDUP(57.5, -1)	60	Rounds 57.5 to one decimal place to the left of the decimal point.
=ROUNDUP(671.3,-2)	700	Rounds 671.3 to two decimal places to the left of the decimal point.
=ROUNDUP(1.78,0)	2	Rounds 1.78 up to zero decimal places.
=ROUND(-70.45,-2)	-100	Rounds -70.45 to the nearest multiple of 100.

ROUNDDOWN Function

The ROUNDOWN function rounds a number down, towards zero.

Syntax

ROUNDDOWN(number, num_digits)

Arguments

Argument	Description
Number	Required. This argument is for the number that you want to round down.
Num_digits	Required. The number of decimal places you want to round the number down to.

Remarks

- ROUNDDOWN works like ROUND except that it always rounds a number down.

- *Number* is rounded down to the specified number of decimal places if num_digits is greater than 0 (zero).

- *Number* is rounded down to the nearest integer if num_digits is 0.

- *Number* is rounded down to the left of the decimal point if num_digits is less than 0.

Examples

In the following examples, ROUNDOWN is applied to several values. The table displays the formula, the result, and a description of the outcome.

Formula	Result	Description
=ROUNDDOWN(3.15, 1)	3.1	Rounds 3.15 down to one decimal place.
=ROUNDDOWN(4.149, 0)	4	Rounds 4.149 down to zero decimal places.
=ROUNDDOWN(-2.475, 2)	-2.47	Rounds -2.475 down to two decimal places.
=ROUNDDOWN(57.5, -1)	50	Rounds 57.5 down to one decimal place to the left of the decimal point.
=ROUNDDOWN(671.3,-2)	600	Rounds 671.3 down to the nearest multiple of 100.
=ROUNDDOWN(1.78,0)	1	Rounds 1.78 down to zero decimal places.
=ROUNDDOWN(-71.45,-1)	-70	Rounds -71.45 down to the nearest multiple of 10.

SQRT Function

This function returns a positive square root of any number.

Syntax

SQRT(number)

Argument	Description
Number	Required. This is the number for which you want to calculate the square root. If *number* is negative, the function returns an error value (#NUM!).

Example

The SQRT function has been applied to the following numbers.

	A	B
	Number	Square root
1	16	4
2	6602	81.25269226
3	4414	66.43794097
4	5788	76.07890641
5	1216	34.87119155
6	0	0
7	1	1
8	820	28.63564213
9	852	29.18903904
10	6358	79.73706792
11	924	30.39736831
12	8689	93.21480569
13	6614	81.32650245
14	-10	#NUM!
15	4163	64.52131431
16	8942	94.56214888
17	2628	51.26402247
18	4010	63.3245608
19	9465	97.28823156

Formula in B2: =SQRT(A2)

CHAPTER 5: STATISTICAL FUNCTIONS

You can access the statistical functions in Excel by clicking on the More Functions button on the Formulas tab. On the drop-down menu, highlight the Statistical option to display a list of all the statistical functions in alphabetical order. The statistical functions in Excel range from everyday statistical functions like AVERAGE, MIN, MAX etc. to more specialized functions used by statisticians.

In this chapter, we'll cover functions that enable you to:
- Calculate the average, min, max and median of values in a range.
- Use a specific criterion to determine which values to aggregate.
- Use multiple criteria to determine which values to aggregate.
- Count the number of values in a range of cells that meet a certain condition.
- Count the number of values in a range that meet multiple criteria.
- Count the number of cells that contain numbers in a range or table.
- Count the number of empty cells in a range or table.

COUNT Function

The COUNT function will count the number of cells that contain numbers in a range, or a list of numbers provided as arguments. The COUNT function only counts populated cells. For example, if you have a range with 20 cells, and only 5 of the cells have numbers, the count function will return 5.

Syntax

COUNT(value1, [value2], ...)

Arguments

Argument	Description
Value1	Required. The first range within which you want to count numbers.
Value2	Optional. Additional cell references or ranges in which you want to count numbers. You can have a maximum of 255 arguments for this function.

Remarks

- You can have a maximum of 255 arguments for this function. Each argument could be a number, a cell reference, or a range.

- The COUNT function counts numbers, dates, or text representations of numbers (i.e. a number enclosed in quotation marks, like "1").

- Error values or text that cannot be translated into numbers are not counted.

- Use the COUNTA function if you want to count text, logical values or error values.

- Use the COUNTIF function or the COUNTIFS function if you want to count only numbers that meet a specific condition.

Example

In this example, we use the COUNT function to count the values in two ranges.

The formula is:

=COUNT(A3:D20,F3:I20)

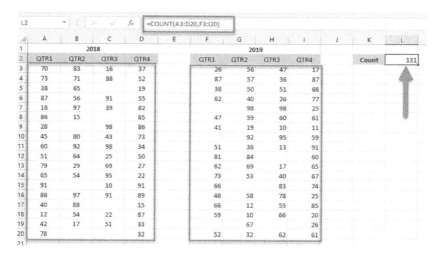

This is a simple formula with two arguments to represent the two ranges in which we want to count values: A3:D20 and F3:I20. Note that the blank cells are not counted.

COUNTIF Function

The COUNTIF function is a combination of a statistical function and a logical function. It allows you to count the number of cells that meet a criterion. For example, you can count only the values in a list of orders that exceed $1,000.

Syntax

COUNTIF(range, criteria)

Arguments

Argument	Description
range	Required. This is the group of cells that you want to count. This argument can contain numbers, a named range, or references that contain numbers.
criteria	Required. This is the condition that is used to determine which cells will be counted. This can be a cell reference, text, expression, or function. For example, you can use a number like 40, a logical comparison like ">=40", a cell reference like D10, or a word like "bolts".

Remarks

- If *criteria* is text or includes logical or mathematical symbols, for example, greater than (>), it must be enclosed in double-quotes ("). If *criteria* is a numeric value, quotation marks are not required.

Example

In this example, we're using COUNTIF to count all Sales over $5,000.

The formula we use is:

=COUNTIF(B2:B11,">5000")

	A	B	C	D	E
1	Salesperson	Sales	Commission		
2	Bruce	$2,635	$132		
3	Louis	$7,227	$361		
4	Earl	$4,426	$221		
5	Sean	$4,774	$239		
6	Benjamin	$9,829	$491		
7	Joe	$20,000	$1,000		
8	Shawn	$2,459	$123		
9	Kenneth	$11,300	$565		
10	Cynthia	$2,566	$128		
11	Susan	$10,894	$545		
12					
13	Report				
14	Count of sales over $5,000		5		
15	Count of commissions over $200		7		

The first argument is the range we want to count - **B2:B11**.

The second argument is the criteria - greater than $5,000 (">£5000").

Note that the criteria is included in quotes because it includes a logical symbol.

Other examples

In the following examples, we have a table of data which we query with different COUNTIF formulas. The formulas, results and descriptions are shown below.

	A	B	C
	Product	**Orders**	
1			
2	Tea	9	
3	Pears	20	
4	Peaches	21	
5	Pineapple	30	
6	Cherry Pie Filling	6	
7	Green Beans	10	
8	Corn	5	
9	Peas	10	
10	Tuna Fish	12	
11	Tea	5	
12	Tea	12	
13	Peaches	10	
14	Peas	2	

(A2 = Tea)

Formula 1	
Formula	=COUNTIF(A2:A14,"Tea")
Result	3
Description	Counts number of cells with tea.

Formula 2	
Formula	=COUNTIF(A2:A14,A4)
Result	2
Description	Counts the number of cells with peaches (the value in A4).

Formula 3	
Formula	=COUNTIF(A2:A14,A2)+COUNTIF(A2:A14,A3)
Result	4
Description	Counts the number of teas and pears in A2:A14.

Formula 4	
Formula	=COUNTIF(B2:B14,">20")
Result	2
Description	Counts the number of values in cells B2:B14 greater than 20.

Formula 5	
Formula	=COUNTIF(B2:B14,"<>"&B7)
Result	10
Description	Counts the number of cells with a value not equal to 10 in cells B2:B14. The ampersand (&) is used for concatenation.

Formula 6	
Formula	=COUNTIF(A2:A14,"T*")
Result	4
Description	Counts the number of items starting with T in cells A2:A14.

COUNTIFS Function

The COUNTIFS function enables you to count values in multiple ranges using multiple criteria to determine what values to count.

Syntax

COUNTIFS(criteria_range1, criteria1, [criteria_range2, criteria2]...)

Arguments

Argument	Description
criteria_range1	Required. The first range you want to evaluate using the associated criteria, which is criteria1.
criteria1	Required. This is the first criteria and it pairs with criteria_range1. It could be a number, cell reference, expression, or text that define which cells will be counted. For example, criteria can be expressed as 40, ">=40", D10, "bolts", or "40".
criteria_range2, criteria2, ...	Optional. Additional ranges and criteria pairs. You can have a total of 127 range/criteria pairs.

Remarks

- Each additional range must have the same number of rows and columns as *criteria_range1*. The ranges do not have to be adjacent to each other.

- If the criteria argument points to an empty cell, the COUNTIFS function treats the empty cell as a 0 value.

- If you are testing for text values, for example, "apples", make sure the criterion is in quotation marks.

- You can use wildcard characters like the question mark (?) and asterisk (*) in your criteria to enable you to find matches that are similar but not the same. The question mark matches any single character and the asterisk matches a sequence of characters. To find a character like a question mark or asterisk, type a tilde sign (~) in front of the character.

Example

In the following example, we want to count the number of people for each state with 40 or more orders. This problem requires us to use two criteria to evaluate two columns. We will be using the state name and ">=40" to determine which records meet our criteria.

We apply the following formula to solve the problem:

=COUNTIFS($B$2:$B$12,F2,$C$2:$C$12,G2)

	A	B	C	D	E	F	G	H
1	Name	State	No. Orders	Sales		States	Orders	# People
2	Bruce	New York	51	$74,298		New York	>=40	2
3	Louis	New York	39	$46,039		Texas	>=40	1
4	Earl	Washington	60	$65,252		California	>=40	1
5	Sean	Washington	100	$61,847		Washington	>=40	2
6	Benjamin	Texas	28	$33,340				
7	Joe	California	31	$95,778				
8	Shawn	Texas	35	$58,808				
9	Kenneth	California	39	$52,593				
10	Cynthia	California	51	$42,484				
11	Susan	Texas	80	$44,390				
12	Dav	New York	70	$66,109				
13								

Formula explanation:

=COUNTIFS($B$2:$B$12,F2,$C$2:$C$12,G2)

- The Criteria_range1 argument references the State column **B2:B12** (an absolute reference has been used - $B$2:$B$12).

  Tip: To convert a cell reference to an absolute reference, select the reference in the formula bar and press the F4 key. You can also type in the dollar signs manually, but it is faster and less error-prone to use F4. An absolute reference ensures the referenced cells do not change relatively when the formula is copied to other cells.

- The Criteria1 argument is **F2**. This is a reference to the State we want to use as our criteria. A cell reference has been used for this argument to make it easier to change.

Also, this argument has been entered as a relative reference because we want it to change relatively as we copy the formula to other cells.

- The *Criteria_range2* is the *No. Orders* column (**$C$2:$C$12**). We will be using our second criteria to evaluate this column. Again, use the F4 key to make it an absolute reference.

- The *Criteria2* argument is **G2** (>=40). A cell reference has been used for this argument to make it easier to change.

We enter the formula in cell **H2** and then copy it down the column to count the number of people with orders that match the criteria for each state.

COUNTA Function

The COUNTA function counts the number of cells that are not empty in a group of cells or range. The difference between the COUNTA and COUNT is that COUNTA counts all cells containing an entry, including empty text ("") and even error values. COUNT, on the other hand, only counts cells that contain numeric values.

Syntax

COUNTA(value1, [value2], ...)

Arguments

Argument	Description
value1	Required. The first argument represents the range in which you want to count cells with an entry.
value2, ...	Optional. You can have additional value arguments up to a maximum of 255 arguments in total.

Remarks

- If you want to count only cells that contain numeric values use the COUNT function.

- Use the COUNTIF function or the COUNTIFS function if you only want to count cells that meet a certain criterion.

Example

In the following example, we use the COUNTA function to count cells with entries in our range of cells. The group of cells containing our data, **A14:D14**, is a named range called *Orders_Range*.

The COUNTA function is demonstrated next to other functions like COUNT and COUNTBLANK to show the difference in the results.

Formula: =COUNTA(Orders_Range)

Result: 37

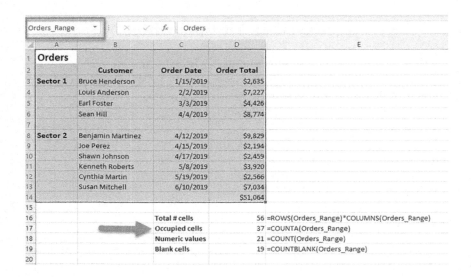

COUNTBLANK Function

The COUNTBLANK function is used to count the number of empty cells in a range.

Syntax

COUNTBLANK(range)

Argument	Description
range	Required. The first argument represents the range in which you want to count the blank cells.

Cells with formulas that return an empty string ("") are also counted. Cells with 0 (zero) are not counted.

Example

In the following example, we use the COUNTBLANK function to count the blank cells in the range **A14:D14** named *Orders_Range*.

Formula: =COUNTBLANK(Orders_Range)
Result: 19

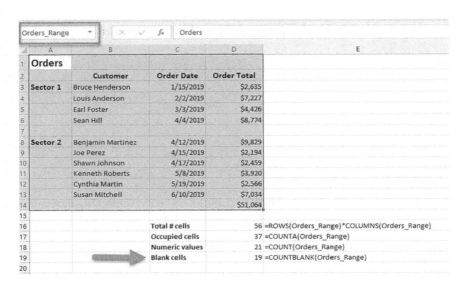

AVERAGE Function

The AVERAGE function is one of the widely used aggregate functions in Excel. It returns the average of the arguments. The average is the arithmetic mean of a series of numbers and is calculated by adding up the numbers and then dividing by the count of those numbers.

Syntax

AVERAGE(number1, [number2], ...)

Arguments

Argument	Description
Number1	Required. The first cell reference, range or number for which you want to calculate an average.
Number2, ...	Optional. Additional cell references, ranges or numbers for which you want to calculate an average, up to a maximum of 255.

Remarks

- Arguments can be numbers, named ranges, or cell references that contain numbers.

- If any of the cells referenced in the arguments contain an error value, AVERAGE returns an error.

- Text, logical values, and empty cells are ignored, however, cells with the value zero (0) are included.

- Use the AVERAGEA function if you want to include logical values and text representations of numbers as part of the calculation.

- Use AVERAGEIF and AVERAGEIFS if you want to calculate the average of only the values that meets some criteria you've set.

Example

In the example below, we use the AVERAGE function to calculate the average of the scores in range B2:C19.

Formula: =AVERAGE(B2:C19)

F1				fx	=AVERAGE(B2:C19)	
	A	B	C	D	E	F
1		Subject 1	Subject 2		Average score	51.86
2	Bruce	0	55			
3	Louis	57	61			
4	Earl	51	47			
5	Sean	74	74			
6	Benjamin	50	50			
7	Joe	30	52			
8	Shawn	95	N/A			
9	Kenneth	8	70			
10	Cynthia	30	45			
11	Susan	57	40			
12	John	67	76			

AVERAGEIF Function

The AVERAGEIF function is a combination of a statistical function and a logical function. AVERAGEIF returns the average (or arithmetic mean) of all the cells in a range that meet a specified condition.

Syntax

AVERAGEIF(range, criteria, [average_range])

Arguments

Argument	Description
Range	Required. A reference to one or more cells to average. This argument can include numbers, cell references, or named ranges.
Criteria	Required. This is a logical test that determines which cells are included in the average.
Average_range	Optional. The actual set of cells to average if not the cells in the *range* argument. If this argument is omitted, *range* is used.

Remarks

- Cells in range that contain logical values like TRUE or FALSE are ignored.

- AVERAGEIF will return an error (#DIV0!) if *range* is a blank or text value.

- If a cell in criteria is empty it is treated as a zero (0) value.

- AVERAGEIF returns the #DIV/0! error value if no cells in the range meet the criteria.

- You can use wildcard characters like the question mark (?) and asterisk (*) in your criteria to enable you to find matches that are similar but not the same. A question mark matches any single character while an asterisk matches a sequence of characters. To find a character like a question mark or asterisk, type a tilde sign (~) in front of the character.

- *Average_range* does not necessarily need to be the same number of rows and columns as *range*. The cells that are averaged are determined by using the top-left cell in *average_range* as the first cell, and then including cells that match the same number of rows and columns in *range*. See the examples below:
    - If the *range* is A1:A10 and *average_range* is B1:B10, then the actual cells evaluated would be B1:B10.
    - If range is A1:A10 and *average_range* is B1:B5, then the actual cells evaluated would be B1:B10.
    - If range is A1:B5 and *average_range* is C1:C3, then the actual cells evaluated would be C1:D5.

Example

In the following example, we use the AVERAGEIF function to calculate the average exam scores for students per subject. We want to group the data by *Subject* (for example, Biology, Chemistry, Maths etc.) and average each group by *Score*.

The range we will be using to select the data - B2:B16, is different from the range we want to actually average - C2:C16.

EXCEL 2019 FUNCTIONS

F2				fx	=AVERAGEIF($B$2:$B$16,E2,$C$2:$C$16)	
	A	B	C	D	E	F
1	Student	Subject	Score		Average per subject	
2	Bruce	Maths	55		Maths	56.2
3	Louis	Chemistry	61		Chemistry	50.0
4	Earl	Biology	47		English	68.0
5	Sean	English	74		Biology	43.5
6	Benjamin	Maths	50			
7	Joe	Chemistry	52			
8	Shawn	Biology	40			
9	Kenneth	English	70			
10	Cynthia	Maths	45			
11	Susan	Chemistry	40			
12	John	Maths	76			
13	Bruce	English	60			
14	Louis	Maths	61			
15	Earl	Chemistry	47			
16	Kenneth	Maths	50			
17						

Formula explanation:

=AVERAGEIF($B$2:$B$16,E2,$C$2:$C$16)

- The **Range** argument references the Subject column B2:B16 (this has been set to absolute reference - **$B$2:$B$16**).

  Tip: To convert a cell reference to an absolute reference, select the reference in the formula bar and press the F4 key. You can also type in the dollar signs manually, but it is faster and less error-prone to use F4. An absolute reference ensures the referenced cells do not change relatively when the formula is copied to other cells.

- The **Criteria** argument is **E2**. This is a reference to the subjects we want to use as our criteria. Instead of directly entering this value into the formula, a cell reference has been used to make it easier to change. This argument is a relative reference (the default) because we want the cell to change relatively as we copy the formula to other cells.

- The **Average_range** is C2:C16 (which is **$C$2:$C$16** as an absolute reference). This is the range for which we want to calculate the average of values that meet our criteria. Use the F4 key to make it an absolute reference.

We enter the formula in cell F2 to return the Maths average. Then the Fill Handle of the cell was used to copy the formula to cells F3:F5 which displays the average for the other subjects

AVERAGEIFS Function

The AVERAGEIFS function returns the average (arithmetic mean) of all cells that meet specific criteria you specify. This function allows you to specify several pairs of criteria to select the data that is included in the average. An IFS function enables you to create several range/criteria pairs used to select the data that meet the criteria.

Once items that meet the criteria have been identified, the average of the corresponding values in the main range is calculated. You can have up to a maximum of 127 range/criteria pairs as you can only have 255 arguments in an Excel function.

Syntax

AVERAGEIFS(average_range, criteria_range1, criteria1, [criteria_range2, criteria2], ...)

Arguments

Argument	Description
Average_range	Required. This is the range of cells for which you want the average calculated.
Criteria_range1	Required. The range that is evaluated using *Criteria1*. This is part of the first range/criteria pair.
Criteria1	Required. This is the criteria used to evaluate *criteria1_range* to select matching data. For example, criteria can be entered as 40, ">40", C6, "bolts", or "125".
Criteria_range2, criteria2, ...	Optional. You can have additional range/criteria pairs, up to a maximum of 127 total pairs.

Example

In this example, we have a list of orders from different sales reps for several states. We want to find the average sales per state for entries that are greater than or equal to 10 orders (>=10).

We apply the following formula to solve the problem:

=AVERAGEIFS($D$2:$D$12,$B$2:$B$12,F2,$C$2:$C$12,G2)

	A	B	C	D	E	F	G	H
1	Name	State	# of Orders	Sales		States	Orders	Average Sales on 10 or more orders
2	Bruce	New York	12	$74,298		New York	>=10	$70,204
3	Louis	New York	5	$46,039		Texas	>=10	$58,808
4	Earl	Washington	15	$65,252		California	>=10	$52,593
5	Sean	Washington	11	$61,847		Washington	>=10	$63,550
6	Benjamin	Texas	9	$33,340				
7	Joe	California	3	$30,000				
8	Shawn	Texas	20	$58,808				
9	Kenneth	California	12	$52,593				
10	Cynthia	California	8	$42,484				
11	Susan	Texas	2	$20,000				
12	Dav	New York	10	$66,109				

Formula explanation:

=AVERAGEIFS($D$2:$D$12,$B$2:$B$12,F2,$C$2:$C$12,G2)

- The *Average_range* argument references the Sales column D2:D12 (an absolute reference has been used - **$D$2:$D$12**). This is the column for which we want to calculate the average.

    Tip: To convert a cell reference to an absolute reference, select the reference in the formula bar and press the F4 key. You can also type in the dollar signs manually, but it is faster and less error-prone to use F4. An absolute reference ensures the referenced cells do not change relatively when the formula is copied to other cells.

- The *Criteria_range1* is B2:B12 (an absolute reference has been used - **$B$2:$B$12**).

- The *Criteria1* argument is **F2**. This is a reference to the state we want to use as our criteria. A cell reference has been used for this argument to make it easier to change.

    This has been left as a relative reference (default) because we want it to change as we copy the formula to other cells.

- The *Criteria_range2* argument is the **# of Orders** column, C2:C12. We will be using *Criteria2* to select the orders that meet the criteria from this range. An absolute reference has been used - **$C$2:$C$12**.

- The *Criteria2* argument is cell **G2** which represents our criteria (>=10). This argument is a matching pair for *Criteria_range2*. A cell reference has been used to make it easier to update with different criteria values.

The formula is entered in cell **H2** and then the Fill Handle of the cell is used to copy the formula to H3:H5. This calculates the average for the other states.

MAX, MIN, MEDIAN Functions

The MAX, MIN and MEDIAN functions are some of the most commonly used functions in Excel and are very similar in their arguments and how they're used. MAX returns the largest number in a specified set of values. MIN returns the smallest number in a set of values. MEDIAN returns the median which is the number in the middle of a set of numbers.

Syntax

Max function: MAX(number1, [number2], ...)

Min function: MIN(number1, [number2], ...)

Median function: MEDIAN(number1, [number2], ...)

Arguments – similar for all three functions

Argument	Description
Number1	Required. The first argument is required and can be a number, range, array, or reference that contain numbers.
number2, ...	Optional. You can have additional numbers, cell references, or ranges up to a maximum of 255 arguments which you want to evaluate.

Remarks

- The functions will return 0 (zero) if the arguments contain no numbers.

- If an argument is a reference or an array, only numbers in that reference or array are used. Logical values, text values, empty cells in the reference or array are ignored.

- The functions will return an error if arguments contain error values or text that cannot be translated into numbers.

- Text representations of numbers and logical values that you directly type into the arguments list are counted.

EXCEL 2019 FUNCTIONS

- For the MEDIAN function, if there is an even number of numeric values in the set, it calculates the average of the two numbers in the middle.

- Use the MAXA and MINA functions if you want to include logical values and text representations of numbers as part of the result for MAX and MIN. You can search for the MAXA or MINA via the **Insert Function** command on the Formulas tab on the Excel ribbon.

Example

In the example below, we want to show the maximum, minimum, and median values for the Sales column (D2:D12) in our table.

The following formulas return the desired results:

- MAX(D2:D12)
- MIN(D2:D12)
- MEDIAN(D2:D12)

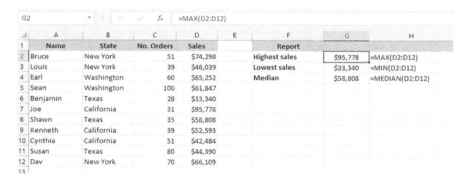

To add more cell references or ranges to the arguments you simply separate them with a comma, for example, MAX(C1:C5, G1:G5).

MAXIFS, MINIFS Functions

The MAXIFS and MINIFS functions are an extension of the MAX and MIN functions to include a conditional component in their functionality. MAXIFS returns the maximum value of all cells that meet the specified criteria. MINIFS returns the minimum value of all cells that meet the specified criteria. You can specify more than one set of criteria to determine which data is selected to be part of the evaluation.

An IFS function enables you to create several range/criteria pairs used to narrow down the data to only those that meet the criteria. Once items that meet the criteria have been identified, the minimum or maximum of the corresponding values in the main range is calculated.

You can have up to a maximum of 127 range/criteria pairs as you can only have 255 arguments in an Excel function.

Note: These functions are new in Excel 2019 so will not be available in older versions of Excel. If you are subscribed to Office 365, make sure you have the latest version of Excel installed.

Syntax

MAXIFS

　　MAXIFS(max_range, criteria_range1, criteria1, [criteria_range2, criteria2], ...)

MINIFS

　　MINIFS(min_range, criteria_range1, criteria1, [criteria_range2, criteria2], ...)

Arguments – similar for both functions

Argument	Description
max_range (MAX function) min_range (MIN function)	Required. The actual range of cells for which we want the maximum or minimum value determined.

criteria_range1	Required. The range that is evaluated using *criteria1*. This is part of the first range/criteria pair.
criteria1	Required. This is the criteria used to determine which cells in *criteria_range1* will be part of the calculation. This can be a number, expression, or text. For example, criteria can be entered as 40, ">40", C6, "bolts", or "125".
criteria_range2, criteria2, ...	Optional. You can have additional range/criteria pairs, up to a maximum of 127 total pairs.

Remarks

- The max_range (or min_range) and criteria_range arguments must have the same number of rows and columns, otherwise, these functions return the #VALUE! error.

- The range we use to filter the data does not necessarily have to be the same range that we want to generate the max or min value from.

Example

In this example, we want to produce reports that show the minimum and maximums sales per state. However, we only want to evaluate entries with 10 or more orders (>=10). So, we have two criteria that we want to use to determine the data to be evaluated.

Formulas

We use the following formulas to return the desired results.

Maximum:
=MAXIFS($D$2:$D$12,$B$2:$B$12,F3,$C$2:$C$12,G3)

Minimum:
=MINIFS($D$2:$D$12,$B$2:$B$12,F10,$C$2:$C$12,G10)

Formula explanation

We have used identical cell references and criteria arguments for both functions, so they can be described together.

MAXIFS($D$2:$D$12,$B$2:$B$12,F3,$C$2:$C$12,G3)

- The first argument for both functions is a reference to the Sales column, D2:D12. This is the actual range we want to evaluate for the minimum and maximum values. An absolute reference has been used - **$D$2:$D$12**.

  Tip: To convert a cell reference in the formula bar to an absolute reference, select the reference in the formula bar and press the F4 key. You can also enter the dollar signs manually, but it is faster and less error-prone to use F4. An absolute reference ensures the referenced cells do not change relatively when the formula is copied to other cells.

- The *Criteria_range1* argument is the **State** column B2:B12. This is part of the first range/criteria pair we'll use to establish our first condition. An absolute cell reference has been used - **$B$2:$B$12**.

- The *Criteria1* argument is **F2**. This is a cell reference to our first criteria, the name of the state which is "New York" in the case of cell F2. A cell reference has been used to hold the value to make it easier to change in future if we so desire.

  This has been left as a relative reference (default) because we want it to change as we copy the formula to other cells.

- The *Criteria_range2* argument is the **# of Orders** column, C2:C12. This is part of the second range/criteria pair. An absolute reference has been used - **$C$2:$C$12**.

- The *Criteria2* argument is cell **G2** which represents the criteria ">=10". This is part of the second range/criteria pair used to filter the data to be evaluated. A cell reference has been used to make it easier to update with different criteria values.

To display the results, we enter the MAXIFS formula in cell **H2** and use the Fill Handle of the cell to copy the formula down to **H5**. This calculates the maximum sales for the other states.

For the minimum values, we enter the MINIFS formula in cell **H10** and use the Fill Handle to copy the formula down to **H13** to calculate the minimum sales for the other states.

CHAPTER 6: DATE AND TIME FUNCTIONS

The date and time functions can be found in Excel by clicking the Date & Time command button on the Formulas tab on the Ribbon. The drop-down menu lists all the date and time functions in Excel.

Excel stores dates and times as serial numbers internally, for example, 43454.83583. The numbers to the left of the decimal point represent the date, and numbers to the right of the decimal point represent the time. This is what is used to carry out date and time calculations behind the scenes. Any entry that is formatted as a date/time is automatically converted internally into a serial number.

For example, by default, January 1, 1900, is serial number 1, and January 1, 2019 is serial number 43466 because January 1, 2019 is 43466 days after January 1, 1900.

In this chapter, we'll cover functions that enable you to:
- Return the day, month or year from a given date.
- Add or subtract days, months and years from dates.
- Combine different values into a single date.
- Return the number of days, months or years between two dates.
- Convert date values entered as text into recognized Excel dates, for example, in the case of imported data.
- Return the number of whole working days between two dates.
- Return the current date or the date and time.
- Return the decimal number for a given time.

Date Formats

Before delving into the date functions, we need to look at date formats in Excel and how to set cells to different date formats. The default date and time formats used by Excel will be the ones you have set in your regional settings in Windows (or macOS for Macs).

The short date format used in Europe is Day/Month/Year (i.e. dd/MM/yyyy) while in the United States the short date format is Month/Day/Year (i.e M/d/yyyy).

You can change the way dates are displayed in your Excel worksheet regardless of your regional date settings in Windows or macOS.

To change the date format in Excel:

1. Select the cell(s) for which you want to change the date format.
2. Click the dialog box launcher on the Number group on the Home tab to launch the **Format Cells** window.
3. Under **Category**, select **Date**.
4. Under **Locale (location)**, select the locale you want, for example, English (United States).
5. Under **Type**, select the date format you want.
6. To select a different time format, select **Time** under Category and follow the same steps as above to choose a time format.
7. When done, click OK.

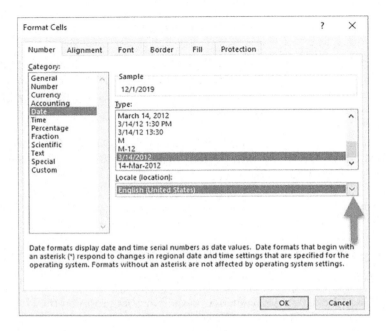

For the examples in this chapter, we will use the United States short date convention **M/d/yyyy**. If you're in a region using the dd/MM/yyyy convention, simply swap the month and day of the dates used in the examples.

DAY, MONTH, YEAR Functions

The DAY, MONTH, YEAR functions are very similar and are usually used together, so will be covered together in this chapter. They all take a single argument which is a serial number representing a date.

DAY returns the day (an integer between 1 to 31) corresponding to a date entered as its argument.

MONTH returns the month (an integer between 1 to 12, representing January to December) corresponding to a date entered as its argument.

YEAR returns the year (as an integer in the range 1900-9999) corresponding to a date entered as its argument.

Syntax

DAY(serial_number)

MONTH(serial_number)

YEAR(serial_number)

Argument	Description
Serial_number	Required. All three functions have the same kind of argument. This argument must be a recognised date. It is the date for the day, month, or year you want to return.
	You can use the DATE function in this argument to ensure a proper date is entered, for example, DATE(2019,4,28). Problems may occur if dates are entered as text.

Remarks

- Dates are stored in Excel as sequential serial numbers to enable calculations to be carried out. For example, by default, 1/1/1900 is serial number 1, and 1/1/2018 is serial number 43101 because 1/1/2018 is 43101 days after 1/1/1900.

- The values returned by the YEAR, MONTH and DAY functions are always Gregorian values regardless of the date format of the argument. For example, if the entered date is Hijri (Islamic Calendar), the values returned by the DAY, MONTH and YEAR functions will be the equivalent in the Gregorian calendar.

Example 1

In this example, we use the DAY, MONTH and YEAR functions to extract the day, month and year from a given date in cell A1, **January 18, 2019**.

Formulas:
=DAY(A1)
=MONTH(A1)
=YEAR(A1)

	A	B	C	D	E
1	1/18/2019		Day	18	=DAY(A1)
2			Month	1	=MONTH(A1)
3			Year	2019	=YEAR(A1)
4					
5					
6					

D1 : =DAY(A1)

Example 2

In this example, we want to add 6 years to December 15, 2017. To calculate the date, we need to use the YEAR, MONTH, and DAY functions as arguments within the DATE function.

When we combine these functions with DATE, we get the following:

	A	B	C	D	E	F	G
1	Contracts						
2	Start Date	Years	End Date				
3	12/15/2017	6	12/15/2023				

Cell C3 formula: =DATE(YEAR(A3)+B3,MONTH(A3),DAY(A3))

Formula Explanation

=DATE(YEAR(A3)+B3,MONTH(A3),DAY(A3))

The *year* argument of the DATE function has **YEAR(A3)+B3**. This will return 2023 (i.e. 2017 + 6). The other functions return the month and day respectively in the *month* and *day* arguments.

To subtract years, use the minus sign (−) in place of the plus sign (+) in the formula.

DATE Function

The DATE function enables you to combine different values into a single date.

Syntax

DATE (year, month, day)

Arguments

Argument	Description
Year	Required. This argument can have one to four digits. Excel uses the date system on your computer to interpret the year argument.
Month	Required. The month argument should be a positive or negative integer between 1 to 12, representing January to December. If the month argument is a negative number (-*n*) the function returns a date that is *n* months back from the last month of the previous year. For example, DATE(2019,-4,2) will return the serial number representing August 2, 2018.
Day	Required. This argument can be a positive or negative integer from 1 to 31, representing the day of the month.

Remarks

- Excel stores dates and times internally as sequential serial numbers to be used in calculations. For example, by default, 1/1/1900 is serial number 1, and 1/1/2018 is serial number 43101 because 1/1/2018 is 43101 days after 1/1/1900.

- If the month argument is greater than 12, the function adds that number of months to the last month of the specified year. For example, DATE(2018,14,4) will return the serial number representing February 4, 2019.

- If Day is greater than the number of days in the specified month, the function adds that number of days to the first day of the next month of the specified date. For, example, DATE(2019,1,36) returns the serial number representing February 5, 2019.

- If Day is less than 1, the function subtracts that number of days from the last day of the previous month of the specified date. For example, DATE(2018,2,-15) will return the serial number that represents January 16, 2018. 15 was subtracted from the 31 days in January which is the previous month to that specified in the function.

- Excel sometimes automatically detects a date entry and formats the cell accordingly. However, if you copied and pasted a date from another source, you may need to manually format the cell to a date to display the date properly.

Tip: To prevent unwanted results, always use four digits for the year argument. For example, "04" could mean "1904" or "2004." Using four-digit years prevents any confusion.

Example 1

In this example, we want to combine values from different cells for the month, day, and year into a date value recognised in Excel.

- Month: 4
- Day: 14
- Year: 2018

When we use the DATE function to combine the values into a single date, we get the following:

=DATE(C2,A2,B2)

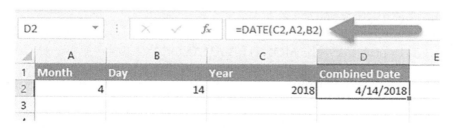

Example 2

This example was covered in a previous chapter but is also applicable here. In this example, we want to add 6 years to December 15, 2017.

To calculate the date, we combine the YEAR, MONTH, and DAY functions with the DATE function. These three functions have been covered in a previous section of this chapter.

- YEAR returns the year corresponding to a date entered as its argument.

- MONTH returns the month corresponding to a date entered as its argument.

- DAY returns the day corresponding to a date entered as its argument.

When we combine these functions with the DATE function, we get the following formula:

=DATE(YEAR(A3)+B3,MONTH(A3),DAY(A3))

Answer: 12/15/2023.

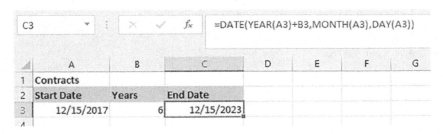

Formula Explanation

=DATE(YEAR(A3)+B3,MONTH(A3),DAY(A3))

The *year* argument of the DATE function has **YEAR(A3)+B3**. This will return 2023 (i.e. 2017 + 6). The other functions return the month and day respectively in the *month* and *day* arguments.

To subtract years, use the minus sign (−) in place of the plus sign (+) in the formula.

Example 3

In this example, we want to add 15 months to December 15, 2017.

Formula:

=DATE(YEAR(A3),MONTH(A3)+B3,DAY(A3))

Answer: 03/15/2019

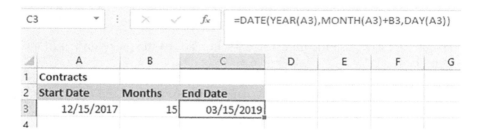

Formula Explanation

In the *month* argument of the DATE function, the syntax, **MONTH(A3)+B3** is what is used to add 15 months to the date. The DATE function will automatically calculate the date from the arguments provided.

To subtract months, use the − sign in place of the + sign in the formula.

Example 4

In this example, we want to add 20 days to December 15, 2017.

Formula:

=DATE(YEAR(A3),MONTH(A3),DAY(A3)+B3)

Answer: 1/4/2018

	A	B	C	D	E	F	G
1	Contracts						
2	Start Date	Days	End Date				
3	12/15/2017	20	01/04/2018				
4							

Formula bar: `=DATE(YEAR(A3),MONTH(A3),DAY(A3)+B3)`

Formula Explanation

The 20 days were added to the DAY function in the *day* argument (i.e. DAY(A3)+B3) of the DATE function. The DATE function accurately returns the End Date based on the input we've provided.

To subtract days, use the minus sign (–) in place of the plus sign (+) in the formula.

To find the difference between two dates you can use the DATEDIF which is covered later in this chapter.

DATEDIF Function

The DATEDIF function calculates the difference between two dates. This function provides one of the easiest ways in Excel to calculate the difference between two dates. It can return the number of days, months, or years between two dates.

DATEDIF is a "hidden" function in Excel because you'll not find it on the list of date functions or when you search for it using the Insert Function dialog box. You must enter it manually any time you want to use it. It is a legacy function from Lotus 1-2-3 but operational on all versions of Excel.

Syntax

DATEDIF(start_date, end_date, unit)

Arguments

Argument	Description
start_date	Required. This argument represents the start date of the period.
end_date	Required. This argument represents the end date of the period.
unit	Required. This argument represents the unit of measurement you want to return - days, months, or years. It should be entered as a string. It can be one of Y, M, D, YM, or YD. "Y" = Calculates the number of years in the period. "M" = Calculates the number of months in the period. "D" = Calculates the number of days in the period. "YM" = Calculates the difference between the months in start_date and end_date. The days and years of the dates are ignored. "YD"= Calculates the difference between the days of start_date and end_date. The years of the dates are ignored.

Note: There is also an "MD" argument that calculates the number of days while ignoring the month and years. However, Microsoft no longer recommends the use of the MD argument in this function because under some conditions it could return a negative number.

Example 1

In the example below, we want to calculate the age of someone born on December 1, 1980.

Formula:

=DATEDIF(A2,TODAY(),"Y")

	A	B
1	Date of Birth	Years
2	12/1/1980	38
3		

We combined the DATEDIF function with the TODAY function to get the desired result. The TODAY function returns today's date, so this formula will always use today's date to calculate the age. The "Y" argument returns the difference in years.

Example 2

To calculate the number of months between two dates we use the "M" argument of the function.

=DATEDIF(A2,B2,"M")

	A	B	C
1	**Start Date**	**End Date**	**Months**
2	12/06/2015	12/01/2017	23

C2: `=DATEDIF(A2,B2,"M")`

DAYS Function

The DAYS function returns the number of days between two dates.

Syntax

DAYS (end_date, start_date)

Arguments

Argument	Description
start_date	Required. This argument represents the start date of the period.
end_date	Required. This argument represents the end date of the period.

Example

In this example, we want to calculate the number of days between two dates, December 1, 2018, and December 1, 2019.

Formula:

=DAYS(B2, A2)

	A	B	C
1	Start Date	End Date	Days
2	12/1/2018	12/1/2019	365
3			
4			

If you're entering the dates directly into the function, you need to enclose them in quotation marks.

For example:

DAYS ("12/01/18", "12/01/2019") will return 365 days.

EDATE Function

The EDATE function allows you to add or subtract months from a given date. EDATE is useful for calculating end dates that are the same day of the month as the start date.

Syntax

EDATE(start_date, months)

Arguments

Argument	Description
Start_date	Required. This argument should be a date representing the start date. It can be a cell reference or a value. Cell references should have the Date format. Use the DATE function for values directly entered. For example, use DATE(2019,1,25) for January 25, 2019. You may get inconsistent results if dates are entered as text.
Months	Required. An integer representing the number of months before or after start_date. A positive value for months returns a date in the future and a negative value returns a date in the past.

Remarks

- Dates are stored in Excel as sequential serial numbers as this is how calculations are carried out internally. For example, by default, 1/1/1900 is serial number 1, and 1/1/2018 is serial number 43101 because 1/1/2018 is 43101 days after 1/1/1900.

- If start_date is not a valid date, EDATE will return an error value (#VALUE!).

- If the months argument is not an integer, it is truncated.

Example

In the following example, we use the EDATE function to calculate the expiry dates for a series of lease contracts with different start dates (A3:A15) and a different lease length (B3:B15).

Formula:

=EDATE(A3,B3)

The formula was entered in cell A3 and copied to the other cells in the column with the Fill handle.

	A	B	C
1	**Property Lease**		
2	Start Date	Length (Months)	Expiry Date
3	1/28/2018	24	1/28/2020
4	4/4/2018	12	4/4/2019
5	4/16/2018	12	4/16/2019
6	5/21/2018	24	5/21/2020
7	5/28/2018	36	5/28/2021
8	10/27/2018	6	4/27/2019
9	11/9/2018	24	11/9/2020
10	12/7/2018	12	12/7/2019
11	12/14/2018	24	12/14/2020
12	2/21/2019	36	2/21/2022
13	5/6/2019	6	11/6/2019
14	7/25/2019	24	7/25/2021
15	11/29/2019	12	11/29/2020

Note that the cells in A3:A15 and C3:C15 were set to the **Date** format so that the dates are displayed properly.

DATEVALUE Function

The DATEVALUE function converts a date that is entered as text to a serial number in Excel that is recognized as a date. The DATEVALUE function is useful in situations where a worksheet contains dates that were imported from another application and seen as text in Excel. You will need to convert the values to recognised dates in Excel to carry out date evaluations.

Once you've converted the values to Excel dates, you can then sort, filter, or add/subtract dates. DATEVALUE returns a serial number internally recognised as a date. To format this number as a date you must apply a **Date** format to the cell.

For example, the formula =DATEVALUE("1/1/2019") returns 43466, which is the serial number for the date, January 1, 2019.

Syntax

DATEVALUE(date_text)

Argument	Description
Date_text	Required. Text that represents a date in an Excel date format, or a reference to a cell that contains text that represents a date in an Excel date format. For example, "1/30/2008" or "30-Jan-2008" are text strings within quotation marks that represent dates.

Remarks

- The date_text argument must represent a date between January 1, 1900, and December 31, 9999. DATEVALUE will return an error if the date_text argument falls outside this range.

- If you omit the year part of the date in the date_text argument, the DATEVALUE function will use the current year from your computer's internal clock.

- Dates are stored in Excel as sequential serial numbers as this is how calculations are carried out internally. For example, by default, 1/1/1900 is serial number 1, and 1/1/2018 is serial number 43101 because 1/1/2018 is 43101 days after 1/1/1900.

- Most functions in Excel automatically convert date values to serial numbers.

Example

In the example below, we convert several date text values to serial numbers using the DATEVALUE function.

	A	B	C	D
1	Date as Text	General number format	Date format (US)	Formula
2	22 May 2011	40685	5/22/2011	=DATEVALUE(A2)
3	5 Jul	43286	7/5/2018	=DATEVALUE(A3)
4	01/01/2019	43466	1/1/2019	=DATEVALUE(A4)
5	April 2019	43556	4/1/2019	=DATEVALUE(A5)

Formula Explanation

=DATEVALUE(A2)

- In the image above, the cells in column A have the text format, the cells in column B have the general number format, and the cells in column C have the date format.

- The DATEVALUE function has been used to convert the text values in A2:A5 to date values in B2:B5. The results are displayed as date serial numbers because the cells have the General number format.

- The DATEVALUE function has been used to convert the text values from A2:A5 to date values in C2:C5. However, in this case, the same results are shown as dates because the Date format has been applied to the range.

NETWORKDAYS Function

The NETWORKDAYS function returns the number of whole working days between two dates. Working days exclude weekends and any dates specified in the *holidays* argument. You can use NETWORKDAYS to calculate employee pay and other benefits based on the number of days worked in a specific period.

Syntax

NETWORKDAYS(start_date, end_date, [holidays])

Arguments

Argument	Description
Start_date	Required. A date that represents the start date.
End_date	Required. A date that represents the end date.
Holidays	Optional. A range, list, or table with one or more dates to be excluded from the working calendar, for example, state holidays, federal holidays and floating holidays.

Remarks

- If you're entering a date directly as an argument, you should use the DATE function to ensure the argument is converted to a date. For example, use DATE(2019,5,23) instead of "May 23, 2019". Problems can occur if dates are entered as text. If you are referencing a date in a cell, ensure the date format is applied to the cell.

- Dates are stored in Excel as sequential serial numbers as this is how calculations are carried out internally. For example, by default, 1/1/1900 is serial number 1, and 1/1/2018 is serial number 43101 because 1/1/2018 is 43101 days after 1/1/1900.

Example

In the example below, we use the NETWORKDAYS function to calculate the number of workdays between the **Project start date** and **Project end**

date of several projects. We also provide a range called **Holiday_range** as the optional *Holidays* argument. **Holiday_range** contains the holiday dates we want to exclude from the count of workdays.

Formula:

=NETWORKDAYS(A2,B2,Holidays_range)

	A	B	C	D
1	Project Start date	Project End date	Work days	
2	2/1/2018	2/1/2019	261	=NETWORKDAYS(A2,B2,Holidays_range)
3	6/1/2018	6/1/2019	259	=NETWORKDAYS(A3,B3,Holidays_range)
4	12/1/2018	12/1/2019	257	=NETWORKDAYS(A4,B4,Holidays_range)
5				
6	Holidays			
7	1/15/2019			
8	2/25/2019			
9	7/4/2019		Named range: Holidays	
10	12/25/2019			

The answers are displayed in the **Work days** column.

Column D is used to display the formulas in column C2:C4 (Workdays).

Tip: If you want to be able to specify weekend days that are different from the default Saturday and Sunday used in the Gregorian calendar, use the NETWORKDAYS.INTL function instead of NETWORKDAYS.

To access the NETWORKDAYS.INTL function, on the Excel ribbon, navigate to **Formulas > Date & Time > NETWORKDAYS.INTL**.

NOW Function

The NOW function returns the current date and time. It's a straightforward function with no arguments. The function displays the date in the cell using the date and time format of your regional settings. Check the **Date Formats** section of this book for how to change the date format of a cell.

You can use the NOW function in situations where you need to display the current date and time on a worksheet and have it updated every time you open the worksheet. You can also use the NOW function to calculate a date value if you want it to always be based on the current date and time.

Syntax

NOW()

Remarks

- The results of the NOW function are not continuously updated. It only updates when the worksheet is recalculated i.e. when new values or formulas are entered, or a macro that contains the function is run.

- If the cell containing the NOW function was changed to a General format, it would display the current date as a serial number, for example, 43454.83583. Numbers to the left of the decimal point represent the date, and numbers to the right represent the time. For example, the serial number 0.5 represents the time 12:00 noon.

- Excel stores dates and times as sequential serial numbers so that they can be used in calculations internally. For example, by default, 1/1/1900 is serial number 1, and 1/1/2018 is serial number 43101 because 1/1/2018 is 43101 days after 1/1/1900.

Example

In the example below, the NOW function is used in different formulas to display date calculations based on the current date and time.

Formulas:

EXCEL 2019 FUNCTIONS

=NOW()
=NOW()-10.5
=NOW()+10
=NOW()+2.25

Formula	Description	Result
=NOW()	Returns the current date and time	12/20/2018 20:35
=NOW()-10.5	Returns the date and time 10 days and 12 hours ago (-10.5 days ago)	12/10/2018 08:35
=NOW()+10	Returns the date and time 10 days in the future	12/30/2018 20:35
=NOW()+2.25	Returns the date and time 2 days and 6 hours in the future (+2.25 days ago)	12/23/2018 02:35
=NOW()	Returns the current date and time (General Number cell format)	43454.85772

TODAY Function

The TODAY function returns the serial number of the current date. Excel stores dates as serial numbers, however, when you enter this function, the cell is automatically changed to a date format to display the value as a date instead of a serial number. To see the date value as a serial number, you must change the cell format to General or Number.

The TODAY function is useful when you want to display the current date on your worksheet, regardless of when the workbook was opened.

It is also useful for calculating the difference between dates. For example, you can calculate the number of years between two dates by using the TODAY formula in combination with the YEAR function:

= YEAR(TODAY())-1979

The formula uses the TODAY function as an argument for the YEAR function to return the current year. The formula then subtracts 1979 from the current year to return the number of years between 1979 and now.

Syntax

TODAY()

Remarks

- Excel stores dates and times as sequential serial numbers so that they can be used in calculations internally. For example, by default, 1/1/1900 is serial number 1, and 1/1/2018 is serial number 43101 because 1/1/2018 is 43101 days after 1/1/1900.

- If the TODAY function does not update when you open the worksheet, you might need to change the settings in Excel that determine when the workbook recalculates.

    To launch Excel Options, navigate to:
    1. File > Options > Formulas.
    2. Under **Calculation options**, ensure **Automatic** is selected.

EXCEL 2019 FUNCTIONS

Example

In the example below, the TODAY function is used in different formulas to display the current date and to calculate other dates based on today's date.

Formulas:
=TODAY()
=TODAY()+10
=DAY(TODAY())
=MONTH(TODAY())
=YEAR(TODAY())-1979

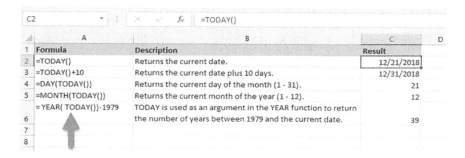

TIME Function

The TIME function returns the decimal number representing a specified time. Excel stores dates and times as serial numbers internally.

Example: 43454.83583

The numbers to the left of the decimal point represent the date and numbers to the right of the decimal point represent the time.

The TIME function will return a decimal number ranging from 0 (zero) to 0.99988426, representing the times from 0:00:00 (12:00:00 AM) to 23:59:59 (11:59:59 PM). If the cell has the General format before the function was entered, the result is formatted as a date to properly display the time instead of a decimal number.

Syntax

TIME(hour, minute, second)

Arguments

Arguments	Descriptions
Hour	Required. This argument can be a number from 0 (zero) to 32767 representing the hour. Any value larger than 23 will be divided by 24 and the remainder will then be treated as the hour value. For example, TIME(29,0,0) = TIME(5,0,0) = .20833 or 5:00 AM.
Minute	Required. This argument can be a number from 0 to 32767 representing the minute. Any value larger than 59 will be divided by 60 and converted to hours and minutes. For example, TIME(0,810,0) = TIME(13,30,0) = .5625 or 1:30 PM.
Second	Required. This argument can be a number from 0 to 32767 representing the second. Any value larger than 59 will be divided by 60 and converted to hours, minutes, and seconds. For example, TIME(0,0,2120) = TIME(0,35,22) = .02456 or 0:35:22 AM

EXCEL 2019 FUNCTIONS

Example

In this example, the range B2:C3 has values for Hour, Minute and Second that we want to use for our calculation. The report in columns E to H shows the results of using the TIME function to evaluate the values in range B2:C3.

Formulas:
=TIME(A2,B2,C2)
=TIME(A3,B3,C3)

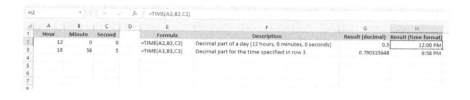

Column G shows the results as decimal values because the cell Number format was set to General.

Column H shows the results as times because Excel automatically applies the Time format to a cell as it knows the TIME function returns a time.

CHAPTER 7: TEXT FUNCTIONS

The text functions in Excel can be found in Excel by clicking the Text command button on the Formulas tab on the Ribbon. The drop-down menu lists all the text functions in Excel. If you work with Excel extensively, there are going to be occasions when you would need to use functions to manipulate text, especially when you work with data imported from other programs.

For example, when you import data into Excel from other applications, you may encounter irregular text spacing or data that's all uppercase. You may want to remove extra spaces from the data or convert uppercase text into proper casing (where only the first letter of each word is in uppercase).

Tip: The Flash Fill command on the Home tab now enables you to automatically carry out many text manipulation tasks for which you would previously use functions. To learn more about Flash Fill, see my book *Excel 2019 Basics*.

In this chapter, we'll cover functions that enable you to:
- Find one text string within a second text string.
- Combine the text from multiple ranges or strings into one string.
- Specify a delimiter as a separator when combining text strings.
- Trim text by removing all extra spaces except single spaces between words.
- Convert text to uppercase or lowercase.
- Capitalize each word in a text string.
- Return the number of characters in a text string.

- Return a specified number of characters from the left, middle, or right of a string.
- Return a portion of a string based on a character or space within the string.

FIND Function

The FIND function is used to locate the starting position of one text string within another text string. It returns the position of the first character of the text your searching for within the second text. The search is case sensitive.

Syntax

FIND(find_text, within_text, [start_num])

Arguments

Argument	Description
Find_text	Required. This is the text you want to find.
Within_text	Required. This is the text containing the text you want to find.
Start_num	Optional. This argument specifies the point, in characters, from which you want to start the search in within_text. The first character in within_text is character number 1. If you omit this argument it will start from the first character in within_text.

Example 1

In this example, we use the FIND function to return the position of different characters in the string "United States". As you can see from the results, the FIND function is case sensitive.

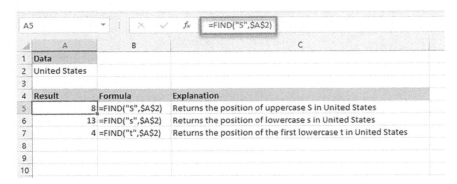

Example 2

The FIND function is most useful when used with another string function in Excel. For example, let's say we want to extract the first part of a reference number like NWTBGM-21. We can use FIND to locate the position of the divider and use the LEFT function to extract the part of the reference we want.

=LEFT(A2,1,FIND("-",A2,1)-1)

FIND returns the position of "-", which is 7 in this case. We need to subtract 1 from this number to remove the divider from the part of the string we're interested in. The LEFT function then uses 6 as the starting point to return the characters in the string starting from right to left. See the section **LEFT, RIGHT Functions** in this book for more on the LEFT function.

FINDB

The FIND function may not be available in all languages. There is an alternative version of this function called FINDB that is available for languages that support the double-byte character set (DBCS) The languages that support DBCS include Japanese, Korean, Chinese Simplified and Chinese Traditional.

FIND, on the other hand, is for computers with a default language that uses the single-byte character set (SBCS). These include English and most of the Western European languages.

Both functions do the same thing. If your system is set to English, you may only have FIND available.

CONCAT Function

The CONCAT function enables you to combine the text from multiple ranges or strings into one string. The function does not provide a delimiter, so you must add that manually in your formula. For example: =CONCAT("Hello"," ","world") will return *Hello world*.

Note: This function was introduced in Excel 2016 as a replacement for the CONCATENATE function. CONCATENATE is still available in Excel for backward compatibility but it is recommended that you use CONCAT going forward.

Syntax

CONCAT(text1, [text2],…)

Arguments

Argument	Description
text1	Required. This argument represents a text item to be joined. It could be a string or a range of cells with text.
[text2, ...]	Optional. Additional text to be joined. You can have up to a maximum of 253 arguments of text items to be joined. Each can be a string or a range of cells with text.

Remarks

- If the resulting string exceeds the cell limit which is 32767 characters, CONCAT returns the #VALUE! error.

- You can use the TEXTJOIN function if you want to include delimiters like spacing and/or commas between the texts you want to combine.

Example

In the example below, we used the CONCAT function in different ways to concatenate text from a range of cells.

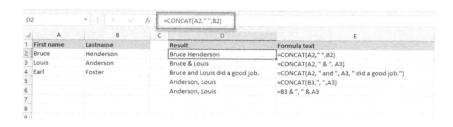

Explanation of formulas

=CONCAT(A2," ",B2)

This formula concatenates the text in A2 and B2 with an empty string in-between represented by the empty string in the formula.

=CONCAT(A2, " & ", A3)

This formula concatenates the text in cells A2 and A3 with an ampersand sign (&) in the middle representing two first names.

=CONCAT(A2, " and ", A3, " did a good job.")

This formula uses the text in cells A2 and A3 to form part of a larger sentence.

=CONCAT(B3,", ",A3)

This formula concatenates the text in cells B3 and A3 with a comma in-between, representing the Last name and First name.

=B3 & ", " & A3

This formula does not use the CONCAT function but achieves the same goal of concatenating two text cells using ampersands.

TEXTJOIN Function

The TEXTJOIN function enables you to combine text values from multiple text strings into one string. The difference between the TEXTJOIN and the CONCAT function is that TEXTJOIN has extra arguments that allow you to specify a delimiter as a separator. It also has an argument you can set to ignore empty cells. If you enter an empty text string in the delimiter, this function will effectively concatenate the ranges.

Note: This feature was introduced in Excel 2019. It should be available to you if you have Office 2019 or if you're an Office 365 subscriber and you have the latest version of Office installed.

Syntax

TEXTJOIN(delimiter, ignore_empty, text1, [text2], ...)

Arguments

Argument	Description
delimiter	Required. This is the delimiter you want to use as a separator for text items in your string. This can be a string, one or more characters enclosed in double-quotes, or a cell reference containing a text string. If this argument is a number, it will be treated as text.
ignore_empty	Required. This should be either TRUE or FALSE. If TRUE it ignores empty cells.
text1	Required. This is the first text item to be joined. It can be a string, a cell reference or a range with several cells.
[text2, ...]	Optional. Additional optional text items to be joined. You can have a maximum of 252 arguments for the text items, including text1. Each can be a string, a cell reference or a range with several cells.

TEXTJOIN will return the #VALUE! error if the resulting string exceeds the cell limit which is 32767 characters.

Example

In the following example, we use TEXTJOIN in C2:C11 to combine the First name and Last name values from A2:A11 and B2:B11. The flexibility provided by TEXTJOIN enables us to swap the order of the names and separate them with a comma.

	A	B	C	D
1	First name	Last name	Combined	Formula
2	Bruce	Henderson	Henderson, Bruce	=TEXTJOIN(", ", TRUE,B2,A2)
3	Louis	Anderson	Anderson, Louis	=TEXTJOIN(", ", TRUE,B3,A3)
4	Earl	Foster	Foster, Earl	=TEXTJOIN(", ", TRUE,B4,A4)
5	Sean	Hill	Hill, Sean	=TEXTJOIN(", ", TRUE,B5,A5)
6	Benjamin	Martinez	Martinez, Benjamin	=TEXTJOIN(", ", TRUE,B6,A6)
7	Joe	Perez	Perez, Joe	=TEXTJOIN(", ", TRUE,B7,A7)
8				
9	Name			
10	Bruce Henderson			
11	Louis Anderson			
12	Earl Foster			
13	Sean Hill			
14				
15	Combined			
16	Bruce Henderson, Louis Anderson, Earl Foster, Sean Hill			=TEXTJOIN(", ",TRUE,A10:A13)
17				

Explanation of formula

=TEXTJOIN(", ", TRUE,B2,A2)

The *delimiter* argument is a comma enclosed in quotes. The *ignore_empty* argument is TRUE because we want to ignore empty cells. The *text1* and *text2* arguments are the cell references B2 and A2, representing the First name and Last name. To populate the other results, we used the Fill Handle of cell C2 to copy the formula down the column.

Tip: You can now use the **Flash Fill** command on the Excel Ribbon to achieve the same results as above. In certain situations, it would be faster to use Flash Fill for this than a formula. If you want more information on Flash Fill, please see my book, *Excel 2019 Basics*.

=TEXTJOIN(", ",TRUE,A10:A13)

The second example uses the TEXTJOIN function to concatenate names in a range of cells (A10:A13) into a single string with a comma used as a separator.

TRIM Function

The TRIM function removes all spaces from a text string except single spaces between words. The aim of TRIM is to remove any extra spaces causing irregular spacing but not the natural spacing between words. The TRIM function is useful when you've imported data into Excel from another application and the text has irregular spacing.

Note: The TRIM function does not remove the non-breaking space commonly used in HTML code or web pages - ** **. To remove this type of space you need to use the Find and Replace function in an HTML editor.

Syntax

TRIM(text)

Argument	Description
Text	Required. The single argument is the text you want to trim. This can be a text value or cell reference.

Example

In the following example, we use the TRIM function to remove all extra spaces from the text values in column A.

	A	B
1	Category	Trimmed
2	Jams, Preserves	Jams, Preserves
3	Dried Fruit & Nuts	Dried Fruit & Nuts
4	Dried Fruit & Nuts	Dried Fruit & Nuts
5	Canned Fruit & Vegetables	Canned Fruit & Vegetables
6	Baked Goods & Mixes	Baked Goods & Mixes
7	Jams, Preserves	Jams, Preserves
8	Baked Goods & Mixes	Baked Goods & Mixes
9		
10		

Cell B2 contains the formula =TRIM(A2)

UPPER, LOWER Functions

The UPPER and LOWER functions work in a similar way and take only one argument. UPPER converts text to uppercase while LOWER converts all uppercase text to lower case.

Syntax

UPPER(text)

LOWER(text)

Argument	Description
Text	Required. The text for which you want to change the case. This argument can be a cell reference or text string.

Example

In the example below, we use the UPPER and LOWER functions to change the case of the text values in column A.

	A	B	C
1	NWTB-1	nwtb-1	=LOWER(A1)
2	NWTCO-3	nwtco-3	=LOWER(A2)
3	Beverages	BEVERAGES	=UPPER(A3)
4	Condiments	CONDIMENTS	=UPPER(A4)
5	Oil	OIL	=UPPER(A5)
6	Jams, Preserves	JAMS, PRESERVES	=UPPER(A6)

Cell B1: =LOWER(A1)

LEN Function

The LEN function returns the number of characters in a text string. The LEN function is useful when used in conjunction with other Excel functions like MID where you can use LEN to return a value for one of its arguments.

Syntax

LEN(text)

Argument	Description
Text	Required. This is a text string or a cell reference containing the text for which you want to find the length. Spaces are counted as characters.

Example

In the following example, we use the LEN function to count the number of characters in an item code. The example also demonstrates how the LEN function can be used in combination with the MID function to return part of a string.

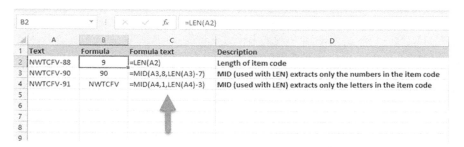

LENB

LENB is a variant of LEN for systems where the double-byte character set (DBCS) language is set as the default language. The languages that support DBCS include Japanese, Traditional Chinese, Simplified Chinese, and

Korean. If your system is not set to the DBCS language set, LENB will just behave like LEN.

MID Function

The MID function enables you to extract a portion of a text string based on a starting position you specify and the number of characters you want to extract.

Syntax

MID(text, start_num, num_chars)

Arguments

Argument	Description
Text	Required. A text string or a cell reference containing the characters you want to extract.
Start_num	Required. This is a number representing the starting position of the first character you want to extract in *text*. The first character in *text* starts with 1, the second is 2 and so on.
Num_chars	Required. This is a number that specifies the number of characters you want to extract from *text*.

Remarks

- If the start_num argument is larger than the length of the string in our text argument, MID will return an empty text ("").

- MID will return the #VALUE! error if start_num is less than 1.

- MID returns the #VALUE! error if num_chars is a negative value.

Example

In the examples below, we use the MID function to extract characters from several text values.

	A	B	C	D
1	01-345-4000	345	=MID(A1,4,3)	Extract the 3 characters in the middle of the serial number
2	01-378-7890	378	=MID(A2,4,3)	
3	01-375-7891	375	=MID(A3,4,3)	
4	01-376-7892	376	=MID(A4,4,3)	
5				
6				
7	NWTCFV-88	88	=MID(A7,8,2)	Extract only the number portion of the item code
8	NWTCFV-89	89	=MID(A8,8,2)	
9	NWTCFV-90	90	=MID(A9,8,2)	
10	NWTCFV-91	91	=MID(A10,8,2)	
11				
12				

Formula description

=MID(A1,4,3)

For this formula, A1 is the cell reference containing the string we want to extract text from - "01-345-4000". The first character we want to extract is 3 which starts at position 4, so we have 4 as our *start_num*. We want to return 3 characters in total, so we have 3 as the *num_chars*.

=MID(A7,8,2)

This formula has A3 as the text argument and 8 as the *start_num* as this is the first character we want to return from the string which has 10 characters. The *num_chars* argument is 2 as this is the number of characters we want to return.

The benefit of using formulas like these is that you create them once and use the fill handle of the first cell to copy the formula to the other cells.

MIDB

MIDB is a variant of MID that counts each double-byte character as two. MIDB is for systems that support the double-byte character set (DBCS). The languages that support DBCS include Japanese, Traditional Chinese, Simplified Chinese, and Korean. If the default language on your computer supports DBCS, you would have MIDB instead of MID but both functions work in a similar way.

PROPER Function

The PROPER function capitalizes the first letter in a text string and converts all other letters in the string to lowercase letters. A text string is a continues stream of characters without spaces. Every letter after a space or punctuation character is capitalized.

Syntax

PROPER(text)

Argument	Description
Text	Required. This can be a string, a cell reference, or a formula that returns a text string that you want to partially capitalize.

Example

In the example below, we use the PROPER function to achieve the desired capitalization for a series of text strings.

=PROPER(A1)

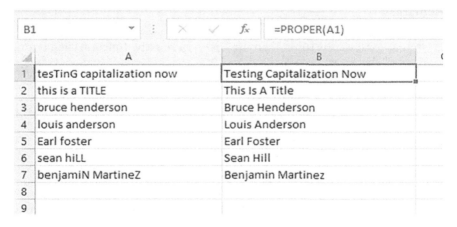

LEFT, RIGHT Functions

The LEFT function returns the leftmost characters in a text string based on the number of characters you specify in one of its arguments. The RIGHT function returns the rightmost characters in a text string based on a number you specify.

Syntax

LEFT(text, [num_chars])

RIGHT(text,[num_chars])

Arguments

Argument	Description
Text	Required. This argument represents the text string with the characters you want to extract.
Num_chars	Optional. This is a number that specifies the number of characters you want to extract from the left (for the LEFT function) or right (for the RIGHT function).

Remarks

- If *num_chars* is larger than the length of *text*, the functions will return all characters in *text*.

- If *num_chars* is omitted, the functions return only the first character for the LEFT function, and only the last character for the RIGHT function.

Example

In the example below, we use the LEFT and RIGHT functions to extract portions of text in different ways.

EXCEL 2019 FUNCTIONS

	A	B	C
	B2		fx =LEFT(A2)

	A	B	C
1	Text	Result	Formula
2	Alabama - AL	A	=LEFT(A2)
3	Alaska - AK	K	=RIGHT(A3)
4	Arizona - AZ	Arizona	=LEFT(A4,7)
5	Arkansas - AR	AR	=RIGHT(A5,2)
6	California - CA	California	=LEFT(A6,FIND("-",A6)-1)
7	Colorado - CO	Colorado	=LEFT(A7,FIND("-",A7)-1)
8	Connecticut - CT	Connecticut	=LEFT(A8,FIND("-",A8)-1)
9	Delaware - DE	DE	=RIGHT(A9,LEN(A9)-(FIND("-",A9)+1))
10	Florida - FL	FL	=RIGHT(A10,LEN(A10)-(FIND("-",A10)+1))
11	Georgia - GA	GA	=RIGHT(A11,LEN(A11)-(FIND("-",A11)+1))
12			

Formula explanations

=LEFT(A2)

This formula takes in cell A2 as the text argument and ignores the optional Num_chars argument. This returns the first character on the left of the string.

=RIGHT(A3)

This formula takes in cell A3 as the text argument and ignores the optional Num_chars argument. Hence the result it returns is the last character in the string (or first from the right).

=LEFT(A4,7)

This formula takes in cell A4 as the text argument and has 7 as the Num_chars argument. It returns "Arizona" which is 7 characters from the left of the string.

=RIGHT(A5,2)

This formula takes in cell A4 as the text argument and has 7 as the Num_chars argument. It returns "AR" which is 2 characters from the right of the string.

=LEFT(A6,FIND("-",A6)-1)

This formula takes in cell A6 as the text argument. We calculate the Num_chars argument by using the FIND function to find and return the position of the dash character (-) in the text.

We then subtract 1 from the result to return the number of characters in the text before the dash. Hence **FIND("-",A6)-1** will return 10. The result is California. This formula will work for any piece of text separated by a dash for which we want to extract the left portion.

=RIGHT(A9,LEN(A9)-(FIND("-",A9)+1))

This formula takes in cell A9 as the text argument. We calculate the Num_chars argument by first using FIND to return the position of the dash character (-) in the text. We then add 1 to move to the position of the first character after the dash (on the right).

The LEN function is used to get the length of the string as we want to subtract the number of characters returned by FIND to give us the number of characters after the dash, which is 2 in this case.

This formula will work for any piece of text separated by a dash for which we want to extract the right portion, regardless of the number of characters after the dash.

LEFTB, RIGHTB Functions

LEFTB and RIGHTB are variants of the LEFT and RIGHT functions that return characters in a text string based on the number of bytes you specify.

RIGHTB/LEFTB are for systems set to a default language that supports the double-byte character set (DBCS). The languages that support DBCS include Japanese, Traditional Chinese, Simplified Chinese, and Korean. If your system has a default language that supports DBCS then you would have LEFTB and RIGHTB in place of LEFT and RIGHT.

If your system has a default language that supports the single-byte character set (SBCS), LEFTB/RIGHTB will behave the same as LEFT/RIGHT, counting 1 byte per character.

CHAPTER 8: FINANCIAL FUNCTIONS

The financial functions in Excel can be accessed by clicking the Financial button on the Formulas tab of the Ribbon. Most of the financial functions in Excel are specialized functions used for financial accounting so before we dive into these functions, we need to cover some financial definitions used in their arguments. Many terms like PV (Present Value), FV (Future Value), PMT (Payment), IPMT (interest payment) etc. come up numerous times in the different financial functions.

In this chapter, we'll cover functions that enable you to:
- Calculate the present value of an investment (or a loan).
- Calculate the future value of an investment.
- Calculate the net present value of an investment taking cash flows into account.
- Calculate the monthly payment for a loan over a given period.
- Calculate the straight-line depreciation of an asset over a given period.
- Calculate the sum-of-years' digits depreciation of an asset over a given period.
- Calculate the fixed-declining balance depreciation of an asset over a given period.
- Calculate the double-declining balance depreciation of an asset over a given period.

Definitions

Annuity
An annuity is a series of regular cash payments over a certain period. For example, a mortgage or a car loan is an annuity. An investment that pays you regular dividends is also an annuity. Most of the functions we will be covering in this chapter are known as annuity functions.

PV (Present Value)
This is the present value of an investment based on a constant growth rate. It is the lump-sum amount that a series of future payments is worth right now.

FV (Future Value)
This is the future value of an investment based on a constant rate of growth. For example, let's say you want to save $25,000 to pay for a project in 20 years, so, $25,000 is the future value. To calculate how much you need to save monthly, you'll also need to factor in an assumed interest rate over the period.

PMT (Payment)
This is the payment made for each period in the annuity. Usually, the payment includes the principal plus interest without any other fees, and it is set over the life of the annuity. For example, a $100,000 mortgage over 25 years at 3% interest would have monthly payments of $474. You would enter -474 into the formula as the *pmt*.

RATE
This is the interest rate per period. For example, if you get a loan at a 6% annual interest rate and make monthly payments, your interest rate per month would be 6%/12.

NPER (Number of periods)
This is the total number of payment periods in the life of the annuity i.e. the term. For example, if you get a 3-year loan and make monthly payments, your loan would have 3*12 periods. Hence, you would enter 3*12 into the formula for the *nper* argument.

Note: The FA, PV, and PMT arguments can be positive or negative values depending on whether you are paying out money or receiving money. If you are paying out money, then the figures will be negative; if you are receiving money then the figures will be positive.

PV Function

The PV function calculates the present value of an investment (or a loan), assuming a constant interest rate. This is the amount that a series of future payments is currently worth. You can use PV with regular payments (such as a mortgage or other loan), periodic payments, or the future value of a lump sum paid now.

Syntax

PV(rate, nper, pmt, [fv], [type])

Arguments

Please see the Definitions chapter above for more a detailed description of these arguments.

Arguments	Description
Rate	Required. This is the interest rate per period.
Nper	Required. The total number of payment periods in an annuity i.e. the term.
Pmt	Required. This is the payment made for each period in the annuity.
	If you omit *pmt*, you must include the *fv* argument.
Fv	Optional. This is the future value of an investment based on an assumed rate of growth.
	If you omit fv, it is assumed to be 0 (zero), for example, the future value of a loan is 0. If you omit fv then you must include the pmt argument.
Type	Optional. This argument is 0 or 1 and indicates when payments are due.
	0 or omitted = at the end of the period.
	1 = at the beginning of the period.

EXCEL 2019 FUNCTIONS

Remarks

- You always need to express the rate argument in the same units as the nper argument. For example, say you have monthly payments on a three-year loan at 5% annual interest. If you use 5%/12 for *rate*, you must use 3*12 for *nper*. If the payments on the same loan are being made annually, then you would use 5% for rate and 3 for nper.

- In annuity functions, the cash paid out (like a payment to savings) is represented by a negative number. The cash you receive (like a dividend payment) is represented by a positive number. For example, a $500 deposit to the bank would be represented by the argument -500 if you are the depositor, and by the argument 500 if you are the bank.

Example

In the example below, we use the PV formula to calculate:

1. The present value of a $500 monthly payment over 25 years at a rate of 1.5% interest.
2. The present value of the lump sum now needed to create $20,000 in 10 years at a rate of 3.5% interest.

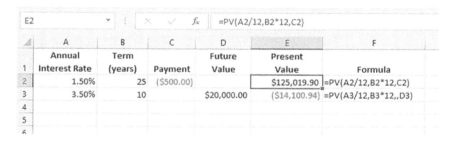

Explanation of Formulas:

=PV(A2/12,B2*12,C2)

As you've probably noticed, the units for *rate* and *nper* have been kept consistent by specifying them in monthly terms, A2/12 and B2*12. The payment (pmt) has been entered in the worksheet as a negative value as this is money being paid out.

=PV(A3/12,B3*12,,D3)

The present value is a negative number as it shows the amount of cash that needs to be invested today (paid out) to generate the future value of $20,000 in 10 years at a rate of 3.5% interest.

FV Function

The FV function calculates the future value (at a specified date in the future) of an investment based on a constant interest rate. You can use FV to calculate the future value of regular payments, periodic payments, or a single lump-sum payment.

Syntax

FV(rate,nper,pmt,[pv],[type])

Arguments

Please see the Definitions in this chapter for more a detailed description of these arguments.

Arguments	Description
Rate	Required. This is the interest rate per period.
Nper	Required. The total number of payment periods in an annuity i.e. the term.
Pmt	Required. This is the payment made for each period in the annuity. If you omit pmt, you must include pv.
Pv	Optional. This is the present value of an investment based on a constant growth rate. If you omit pv, it is assumed to be 0 (zero) and you must include pmt.
Type	Optional. The *type* is 0 or 1 and it indicates when payments are due. 0 (or omitted) = at the end of the period. 1 = at the beginning of the period.

Remarks

- You always need to express the rate argument in the same units as the nper argument. For example, say you have monthly payments on a three-year loan at 5% annual interest. If you use 5%/12 for *rate*, you must use 3*12 for *nper*. If the payments on the same loan are being made annually, then you would use 5% for rate and 3 for nper.

- In an annuity function, cash paid out (like a payment to savings) is represented by as a negative number. The cash you receive (like a dividend) is represented by a positive number. For example, a $500 deposit to the bank would be represented by the argument -500 if you are the depositor, and by the argument 500 if you are the bank.

Example

In the example below, we use the FV function to calculate:

1. The future value of a monthly payment of $200 over 10 months at an interest of 6% per annum.

2. The future value of a lump sum of $1,000 plus 12 monthly payments of $100, at an interest rate of 6%.

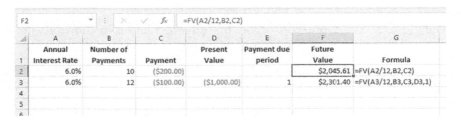

	A	B	C	D	E	F	G
1	Annual Interest Rate	Number of Payments	Payment	Present Value	Payment due period	Future Value	Formula
2	6.0%	10	($200.00)			$2,045.61	=FV(A2/12,B2,C2)
3	6.0%	12	($100.00)	($1,000.00)	1	$2,301.40	=FV(A3/12,B3,C3,D3,1)
4							
5							
6							

Explanation of Formulas:

=FV(A2/12,B2,C2)

Note that the *rate* argument has been divided by 12 to represent monthly payments. The *pmt* argument is a negative value (C2) as this is money being paid out.

=FV(A3/12,B3,C3,D3,1)

This formula has the pmt argument as well as the optional pv argument which represents the present value of the investment. The payment due period is 1 which means the payment starts at the beginning of the period.

NPV Function

The NPV function calculates the net present value which is the present value of cash inflows and cash outflows over a period. It calculates the present value of an investment by applying a discount rate and a series of future payments that may be income (positive values) or payments/losses (negative values).

Syntax

NPV(rate,value1,[value2],...)

Arguments

Argument	Description
Rate	Required. This is the percentage rate of discount over the length of the investment.
Value1	Required. This represents either a payment/loss (negative value) or income (positive value).
value2, ...	Optional: You can have additional values representing payments and income up to a total of 254 value arguments. The length of time between these payments must be equally spaced and occur at the end of each period.

Remarks

- The rate argument in the function might represent the rate of inflation or the interest rate that you might get from an alternative form of investment, for example, a high-yield savings account.

- The value arguments represent the projected income (or loss) values over the period of the investment.

- Ensure you enter the payment and income values in the correct order because NPV uses the order of the value arguments to interpret the order of cash flows.

- The NPV investment begins one period before the date of the first cash flow (value1) and ends with the last cash flow (valueN) in the list of value arguments. If the first cash flow happens at the beginning of the period, you must add it to the result of the NPV function and not include it as one of its value arguments.

- The main difference between NPV and PV is that with PV, the cash flows can start at the beginning or end of the period while for NPV the cash flows start at the beginning of the period. Also, PV has the same cash flow amount throughout the investment while NPV can have different cash flow amounts.

- Arguments that are not numbers are ignored.

Example

In the example below, we are calculating the net present value of an initial investment of $50,000 over the course of five years, considering an annual discount rate of 2.5 percent.

Formula explanation

=NPV(I4,C4:G4)+B4

In the figure above, Year 1 of the investment shows a loss of $1,000, hence, this has been entered as a negative value. The other years of the investment (years two to five) returned a profit, so these were entered as positive values.

The function uses two arguments, the *rate* and *value1*, which references cells C4:G4. The initial investment is added to the result returned by the function rather than being an argument in the function.

The result shows the net present value of the investment over five years is: **$46,727.78.**

PMT Function

The PMT function calculates the payment for a loan on regular payments and a constant interest rate over a period. The PMT function is often used to calculate the repayment of a mortgage with a fixed interest rate.

Syntax

PMT(rate, nper, pv, [fv], [type])

Arguments

Arguments	Description
Rate	Required. This is the interest rate per period.
Nper	Required. This is the total number of payment periods in an annuity i.e. the term.
Pv	Required. This is the present value of a principal or a series of future payments.
Fv	Optional. This is the future value of an investment based on an assumed rate of growth. If you omit fv, it is assumed to be 0 (zero), i.e. the future value of a loan is 0.
Type	Optional. This argument is 0 or 1 and indicates when payments are due. 0 (or omitted) = at the end of the period. 1 = at the beginning of the period.

Remarks

- The payment returned by PMT is for the principal and interest. It does not include taxes, reserve payments, or other fees they may be associated with loans.

- You always need to express the *rate* argument in the same units as the *nper* argument. For example, say you have monthly payments on a three-year loan at 5% annual interest. If you use 5%/12 for *rate*, you must use 3*12 for *nper*. If the payments on the same loan are being made annually, then you would use 5% for rate and 3 for nper.

Tip: To calculate the total amount paid over the duration of the loan, simply multiply the value returned by PMT by the number of payments (nper).

Example

In the example below, we calculate the PMT for two loans:

1. A $10,000 loan over 12 payments at 8.0 percent interest.
2. A $10,000 loan over 60 payments at 4.9 percent interest.

	A	B	C	D	E
1	Annual Interest Rate	Number of payments	Amount of loan	PMT	Formula
2	8.0%	12	$10,000.00	($869.88)	=PMT(A2/12,B2,C2)
3	4.9%	60	$10,000.00	($188.25)	=PMT(A3/12,B3,C3)

Formula explanation

=PMT(A2/12,B2,C2)

The rate argument is a reference to cell A2 divided by 12, to represent the interest rate in monthly terms as nper (cell B2) is also specified in monthly terms. The pv argument takes in C2, which is the present value of the loan $10,000.

Answer: ($869.88)

=PMT(A3/12,B3,C3)

This formula is also for a loan of $10,000, however, the nper is 60 and the rate is 4.9 percent.

Answer: ($188.25)

SLN Function

The SLN function is a depreciation function and calculates the straight-line depreciation of an asset over a period. It depreciates the asset by the same amount each year.

Syntax

SLN(cost, salvage, life)

Arguments

Argument	Description
Cost	Required. This is the initial cost of the asset you're depreciating.
Salvage	Required. This is the value at the end of the depreciation (also referred to as the salvage value of the asset).
Life	Required. This is the number of periods over which the asset is depreciating (also referred to as the useful life of the asset).

Example

In the example below, we have a report calculating the SLN depreciation of a couple of cars with a useful life of 10 years.

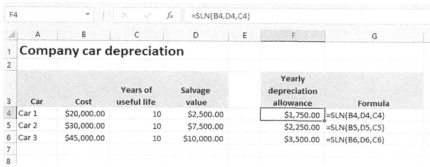

Formula explanation

=SLN(A4,C4,B4)

For Car 1, the *cost* references a cell B4 ($20,000), the *salvage* value references cell D4 ($2,500), and the life is C4 (10 years).

The formula returns $1,750, which is the yearly depreciation allowance to be made for the car. This value would be subtracted from the value of the car when listing this asset in the company's balance sheet.

The formula in F4 was copied down using the fill handle of the cell to calculate the SLN value of the other cars on the list.

SYD Function

The SYD function (sum of years' digits) is a depreciation function that returns the sum-of-years' digits depreciation of an asset over a specified period.

Syntax

SYD(cost, salvage, life, per)

Arguments

Argument	Description
Cost	Required. This is the initial cost of the asset you're depreciating.
Salvage	Required. This is the value at the end of the depreciation (also referred to as the salvage value of the asset).
Life	Required. This is the number of periods over which the asset is depreciating (also referred to as the useful life of the asset).
Per	Required. This is the period and it must be in the same units as life.

Example

In the example below, we use the SYD function to calculate the depreciation of some office equipment over 10 years.

Function arguments:
- Cost = $40,000
- Life = 10 (years)
- Salvage = $1,000

	A	B	C	D	E	F
1	Depreciation of office equipment					
2						
3		Initial Cost	$40,000.00			
4		Life (years)	10			
5		Salvage value	$1,000.00			
6						
7	Year	SYD	Asset value			
8	0	$0.00	$40,000.00			
9	1	$7,090.91	$32,909.09			
10	2	$6,381.82	$26,527.27			
11	3	$5,672.73	$20,854.55			
12	4	$4,963.64	$15,890.91		Cumulative depreciation	
13	5	$4,254.55	$11,636.36			
14	6	$3,545.45	$8,090.91			
15	7	$2,836.36	$5,254.55			
16	8	$2,127.27	$3,127.27			
17	9	$1,418.18	$1,709.09			
18	10	$709.09	$1,000.00			
19						

Cell B9 formula: =SYD($C$3,$C$5,$C$4,A9)

Formula explanation

=SYD($C$3,$C$5,$C$4,A9)

The formula in cell B9 uses absolute references ($C$3, $C$5, and $C$4) for the cost, salvage, and life arguments as these remain the same over the 10-year depreciation period. The *per* argument is a relative reference, cell A9, which changes in relation to the year being calculated.

As you can see from the image above, with the SYD function, the depreciation amount gets progressively smaller, compared to the SLN which is constant over the period.

=C8-SYD($C$3,$C$5,$C$4,A9)

The formulas in the **Asset value** column (C9:C18), subtracts each year's depreciation from the previous year's calculated value of the asset. Hence, this column shows a progressive decrease in the value of the asset over the 10-year period until it gets to the salvage value.

DB Function

The DB function is a depreciation function that uses the fixed-declining balance method to return the depreciation of an asset over a specified period. The fixed-declining balance method calculates the depreciation at a fixed rate.

Syntax

DB(cost, salvage, life, period, [month])

Arguments

Arguments	Descriptions
Cost	Required. This is the initial cost of the asset you're depreciating.
Salvage	Required. This is the value at the end of the depreciation (also referred to as the salvage value of the asset).
Life	Required. This is the number of periods over which the asset is depreciating (also referred to as the useful life of the asset).
Period	Required. This is the period and it must be in the same units as life.
Month	Optional. This is the number of months in the first year of the depreciation if not 12. If this argument is omitted, it is assumed to be 12.

Remarks

- The following formulas are used to calculate depreciation for a period:

    *(cost - total depreciation from prior periods) * rate*

    Where: *rate = 1 - ((salvage / cost) ^ (1 / life))*

- DB uses different formulas to calculate the depreciation for the first and last periods.

First period:

*cost * rate * month / 12*

Last period:

*((cost - total depreciation from prior periods) * rate * (12 - month)) / 12*

Example 1

In the following example, we're calculating the depreciation of an asset over 5 years using the following data:

- Costs = $10,000
- Salvage value = $2,000
- Life = 5 years.

The first year has 12 months so we can omit the month argument.

The formula for the first month will be thus:

=DB(10000, 2000, 5, 1)

Result: $2,750.00

Example 2

In this example, the depreciation is being calculated for an asset that costs $10,000, a salvage value of $2,000, and the useful life is 5 years.

The depreciation is being calculated for the fifth year, and there are 8 months in the first year. The formula for the first month will be thus:

=DB(10000, 2000, 5, 5, 8)

Result: $855.84

Example 3

In this example, we use the SYD function to calculate the depreciation of office equipment with a useful life of 10 years. The initial cost is $40,000 and the salvage value is $1,000.

The first year has only 7 months, so we need to specify that in the *month* argument.

	A	B	C	D	E
			fx =DB($C$3,$C$5,$C$4,A9,$C$6)		
1	Depreciation of office equipment				
2					
3		Initial Cost	$40,000.00		
4		Life (years)	10		
5		Salvage value	$1,000.00		
6		First year (# of months)	7		
7					
8	Year	DB	Asset value		
9	1	$7,186.67	$32,813.33		
10	2	$10,106.51	$22,706.83		
11	3	$6,993.70	$15,713.12		
12	4	$4,839.64	$10,873.48		
13	5	$3,349.03	$7,524.45		
14	6	$2,317.53	$5,206.92		
15	7	$1,603.73	$3,603.19		
16	8	$1,109.78	$2,493.41		
17	9	$767.97	$1,725.44		
18	10	$531.43	$1,194.00		
19					

Formula explanation

=DB($C$3,$C$5,$C$4,A9,$C$6)

The formula in cell B9 uses absolute references ($C$3, $C$5, and $C$4) for the *cost*, *salvage*, and *life* arguments as these remain the same over the 10-year depreciation period.

The *per* argument is a relative reference, cell A9, which changes in relation to the year being calculated.

The *month* argument is an absolute reference, $C$6, which holds a value of 7. This specifies that the first year of the depreciation is 7 months rather than 12. If the first year was 12 months, then this argument could have been omitted.

As you can see from the image above, with the DB function, apart from the first year, the depreciation result is reduced progressively as the value of the asset is reduced.

DDB Function

This DDB function returns the depreciation of an asset for a specified period using the double-declining balance method. The double-declining balance method calculates depreciation at an accelerated rate with the depreciation highest in the first period and decreasing in successive periods.

This function is flexible in that you can change the *factor* argument if you do not want to use the double-declining balance method.

Syntax

DDB(cost, salvage, life, period, [factor])

Arguments

Argument	Description
Cost	Required. This is the initial cost of the asset you're depreciating.
Salvage	Required. This is the value at the end of the depreciation (also referred to as the salvage value of the asset).
Life	Required. This is the number of periods over which the asset is depreciating (also referred to as the useful life of the asset).
Period	Required. This is the period and it must be in the same units as life.
Factor	Optional. This is the rate at which the balance declines. If omitted, the factor is assumed to be 2, which is the double-declining balance method.

Important: The five arguments must be positive numbers.

Remarks

The DDB function uses the formula below to calculate depreciation for a period:

Min((cost - total depreciation from prior periods) * (factor/life), (cost - salvage - total depreciation from prior periods))

Example

In the following example, we use different DDB formulas to return results for the depreciation of a car.

Data:
- Initial Cost: $25,000.00
- Salvage value: $2,500.00
- Life (in years): 10

	A	B	C
1	Depreciation of car		
2			
3	Initial Cost	$25,000.00	
4	Salvage value	$2,500.00	
5	Life (in years)	10	
6			
7	Formula	Result	Explanation
8	=DDB($B$3,$B$4,$B$5*365,1)	$13.70	First day's depreciation. Defaults to factor 2
9	=DDB($B$3,$B$4,$B$5*12,1,2)	$416.67	First month's depreciation
10	=DDB($B$3,$B$4,$B$5,1,2)	$5,000.00	First year's depreciation
11	=DDB($B$3,$B$4,$B$5,1,1.5)	$3,750.00	First year's depreciation using a factor of 1.5
12	=DDB($B$3,$B$4,$B$5,10)	$671.09	Tenth year's depreciation

Cell B8 formula: =DDB($B$3,$B$4,$B$5*365,1)

Explanation of formulas

=DDB($B$3,$B$4,$B$5*365,1)

The formula in cell B8 uses absolute references ($B$3,$B$4, and $B$5*365) for the *cost*, *salvage* and *life*. Life is (10 * 365) because we want to calculate the depreciation in daily units rather than months or years. The period is 1, representing the first day of the life. The factor argument has been omitted so it defaults to 2, hence using the double-declining balance method.

=DDB($B$3,$B$4,$B$5*12,1,2)

First month's depreciation. In this case, the factor argument has been included to specify the double-declining balance method.

=DDB($B$3,$B$4,$B$5,1,2)

The first year's depreciation. Notice that the *life* argument $B$5 has not been multiplied by 12 so the formula will return a result for year 1 as specified in the period argument.

=DDB($B$3,$B$4,$B$5,1,1.5)

This is the first year's depreciation using a factor of 1.5 instead of the double-declining balance method.

=DDB($B$3,$B$4,$B$5,10)

For the final formula, we return the tenth year's depreciation result. Factor has been omitted so it defaults to 2.

AFTERWORD: GETTING MORE HELP WITH FUNCTIONS

In deciding which functions to cover from each category, relevancy to the average user has been taken into consideration. Some Excel functions require specialist knowledge in certain professional areas, for example, Engineering to be of relevance, and these have not been covered here.

To get more help with these specialist functions, press F1 in the Excel window to display the Help panel. Then type "Excel functions" in the search bar. This will give you a list of all the functions in Excel grouped by category or in alphabetical order.

When you identify the function you want, you can visit its details page for a detailed description of the function and its arguments.

You can also visit Microsoft's online help for Excel functions which has the same information as the internal help in Excel.

Web link:
https://support.office.com/en-us/article/excel-functions-alphabetical-b3944572-255d-4efb-bb96-c6d90033e188

APPENDIX: KEYBOARD SHORTCUTS (EXCEL FOR WINDOWS)

The Excel Ribbon comes with new shortcuts called Key Tips. To see Key Tips, press the Alt key when Excel is the active window.

The following table lists the most frequently used shortcuts in Excel 2019.

Keystroke	Action
F1	Opens Excel's Help window
Ctrl+O	Open a workbook
Ctrl+W	Close a workbook
Ctrl+C	Copy
Ctrl+V	Paste
Ctrl+X	Cut
Ctrl+Z	Undo
Ctrl+B	Bold
Ctrl+S	Save a workbook
Ctrl+F1	Displays or hides the ribbon
Delete key	Remove cell contents
Alt+H	Go to the Home tab
Alt+H, H	Choose a fill color

Alt+N	Go to Insert tab
Alt+A	Go to Data tab
Alt+P	Go to Page Layout tab
Alt+H, A, then C	Center align cell contents
Alt+W	Go to View tab
Shift+F10, or Context key	Open context menu
Alt+H, B	Add borders
Alt+H,D, then C	Delete column
Alt+M	Go to Formula tab
Ctrl+9	Hide the selected rows
Ctrl+0	Hide the selected columns

Access Keys for Ribbon Tabs

To go directly to a tab on the Excel Ribbon, press one of the following access keys.

Action	Keystroke
Open the Tell me box on the Ribbon.	Alt+Q
Open the File page i.e. the Backstage view.	Alt+F
Open the Home tab.	Alt+H
Open the Insert tab.	Alt+N
Open the Page Layout tab.	Alt+P
Open the Formulas tab.	Alt+M
Open the Data.	Alt+A
Open the Review.	Alt+R
Open the View.	Alt+W

To get a more comprehensive list of Excel for Windows Shortcut, press **F1** to open Excel Help and type in "Keyboard shortcuts" in the search bar.

GLOSSARY

Absolute reference
This is a cell reference that doesn't change when you copy a formula containing the reference to another cell. For example, $A$3 means the row and column have been set to absolute.

Active cell
The cell that is currently selected and open for editing.

Alignment
The way a cell's contents are arranged within that cell. This could be left, centred or right.

Arguments
The input values a function requires to carry out a calculation.

AutoCalculate
This is an Excel feature that automatically calculates and displays the summary of a selected range of figures on the status bar.

AutoComplete
This is an Excel feature that completes data entry for a range of cells based on values in other cells in the same column or row.

Backstage view
This is the screen you see when you click the File tab on the ribbon. It has a series of menu options to do with managing your workbook and configuring global settings in Excel.

EXCEL 2019 FUNCTIONS

Cell reference
The letter and number combination that represents the intersection of a column and row. For example, B10 means column B, row 10.

Conditional format
This is a format that applies only when certain criteria are met by the cell content.

Conditional formula
A conditional formula calculates a value from one of two expressions based on whether a third expression evaluates to true or false.

Excel table
This is a cell range that has been defined as a table in Excel. Excel adds certain attributes to the range to make it easier to manipulate the data as a table.

Fill handle
This is the plus sign (+) at the lower-right of the selected cell that can be dragged to AutoFill values of other cells.

FillSeries
This is the Excel functionality that allows you to create a series of values based on a starting value including any rules or intervals.

Formula
An expression used to calculate a value.

Formula bar
This is the area just above the worksheet grid that displays the value of the active cell. This is where you enter a formula in Excel.

Function
This is a predefined formula in Excel that just requires input values (arguments) to calculate and return a value.

Named range
A group of cells in your worksheet given one name that can then be used as a reference.

PivotTable
This is an Excel summary table that allows you to dynamically summarise data from different perspectives. PivotTables are highly flexible, and you can quickly adjust them, depending on how you need to display your results.

Quick Access Toolbar
This is a customisable toolbar with a set of commands independent of the tab and ribbon commands currently on display.

Relative reference
Excel cell references are relative references by default. This means, when copied across multiple cells, they change based on the relative position of rows and columns.

Ribbon
This is the top part of the Excel screen that contains the tabs and commands.

Sort
A sort means to reorder the data in a worksheet based on a criterion. So, you could sort in ascending order or in descending order.

Workbook
This is the Excel document itself and it can contain one or more worksheets.

Worksheet
A worksheet is like a page in an Excel workbook.

INDEX

A

absolute reference, 75, 99
ADDRESS, 31
Advanced IF functions, 50
AGGREGATE, 77
AND, 61
Annuity, 169
AVERAGE, 105
AVERAGEIF, 107
AVERAGEIFS, 111

C

cash inflows, 176
cash outflows, 176
CHOOSE, 26
COLUMNS, 36
CONCAT, 152
COUNT, 92
COUNTA, 101
COUNTBLANK, 103
COUNTIF, 94
COUNTIFS, 98

D

DATE, 126
date formats, 121
DATEDIF, 131
DATEVALUE, 138
DAY, 123
DAYS, 134
DB function, 185
DDB function, 189
depreciation, 181, 185, 189, 190
double-byte character set (DBCS), 151
double-declining balance, 189

E

EDATE, 136

F

FIND, 150
FINDB, 151
fixed-declining balance, 185
Flash Fill, 148, 155
FORMULATEXT, 34
future value, 169
FV, 173

G

Gregorian calendar, 124

H

Hijri, 124
HLOOKUP, 19

I

IF, 46
IFERROR, 59
IFS, 53
INDEX, 39
Insert Function, 11, 115, 131
interest rate, 173

L

LEFT, 164
LEFTB, 166
LEN, 159
loan, 179, 180

LOWER, 158

M

MATCH, 22
MAX, 114
MAXA, 115
MAXIFS, 116
MEDIAN, 114
MID, 159, 161
MIDB, 162
MIN, 114
MINA, 115
MINIFS, 116
MOD, 81
MONTH, 123
mortgage, 179

N

Nested IF, 49
NETWORKDAYS, 140
NOW, 142
NPER (Number of payment), 169
NPV, 176

O

OR, 64

P

payment made, 169
PMT, 179
present value, 169
PROPER, 163
PV, 170

R

RANDBETWEEN, 82
rate, 169

RIGHT, 164
RIGHTB, 166
ROUND, 84
ROUNDOWN, 88
ROUNDUP, 86
ROWS, 37

S

SLN, 181
SQRT, 90
SUM, 68
SUMIF, 71
SUMIFS, 74
SWITCH, 57
SYD, 183

T

TEXTJOIN, 154
TIME, 146
TODAY, 144
TRANSPOSE, 29
TRIM, 157

U

UPPER, 158

V

VLOOKUP, 16

W

wildcard characters, 107

Y

YEAR, 123

ABOUT THE AUTHOR

Nathan George is a computer science graduate with several years' experience in the IT services industry in different roles which included Excel VBA programming, Excel training, and providing end-user support to Excel power users. One of his main interests is using computers to automate tasks and increase productivity. As an author, he has written several technical and non-technical books.

OTHER BOOKS BY AUTHOR

Excel XLOOKUP and Other Lookup Functions

Create Easier and More Versatile Lookup Formulas with New Powerful Excel Functions

Do you want to create easier and faster lookup formulas?

XLOOKUP is dynamic array lookup function only introduced in 2020 that will supersede both the VLOOKUP and HLOOKUP functions.

XLOOKUP is easier to use, has more features, and provides greater flexibility in performing lookups in Excel.

This book covers XLOOKUP and other new dynamic array formulas in more depth and with more examples than is practical in a general-purpose Excel book.

After reading this book, you will know how to use XLOOKUP to perform a variety of lookup tasks, from basic to advanced; you will know how to use the new XMATCH function in combination with INDEX to perform complex lookups; you will know how to use the new FILTER and SORT functions to fetch and transform data.

This book also covers the good old VLOOKUP in some depth, if you still need it, depending on the version of Excel you have.

For more details go to:
https://www.excelbytes.com/excel-books

Excel 2019 Basics

A Quick and Easy Guide to Boosting Your Productivity with Excel

A Step-By-Step Approach to Learning Excel Fast!

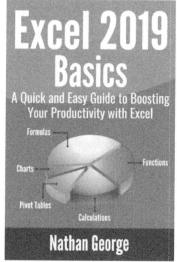

Excel 2019 Basics covers all you need to quickly get up to speed in creating spreadsheets to provide solutions for your data.

If you are new to Excel and the thought of spreadsheets makes your head spin, then you've come to the right place. This book will hold your hand through a step-by-step process in becoming skilled with Excel.

If you already have some Excel skills and you want to skill-up on more advanced topics like functions, Excel tables, pivot tables, and charts, then you've also come to the right place. Excel 2019 Basics goes beyond introduction topics and covers topics like functions, Excel tables, and analysing your data with charts.

The aim of this book is to guide you from beginner to being skilled with Excel within a few short hours.

For more details go to:
https://www.excelbytes.com/excel-books

Excel 2019 Advanced Topics

Leverage More Powerful Tools to Enhance Your Productivity

Whether you have basic Excel skills or you're a power user, *Excel 2019 Advanced Topics* is full of methods and tips that will enable you to take advantage of more powerful tools in Excel to boost your productivity.

Excel 2019 Advanced Topics covers a selection of advanced topics relevant to productivity tasks you're more likely to perform at home or work.

This book does not only show you how to use specific features, but also in what context those features need to be used.

Excel 2019 Advanced Topics explains how to automate Excel with macros, use What-If Analysis tools to create different data scenarios and projections, analyze data with pivot tables and pivot charts; debug and fix formula errors; solve complex data scenarios with advanced functions; use data tools to consolidate data; remove duplicate values from lists; perform financial calculations using specialized finance and accounting formulas; and much more.

For more details go to:
https://www.excelbytes.com/excel-books

Excel 2019 Macros and VBA

An Introduction to Excel Programming

Do you often perform repetitive tasks in Excel that can be time-consuming?

You can automate pretty much any task in Excel with a macro.

If you want to automate Excel, *Excel 2019 Macros and VBA* will be a great resource for you.

We start from the very basics of Excel automation, so you do not need any prior experience of Excel programming.

You will learn how to automate Excel using recorded macros as well as Visual Basic for Applications (VBA) code. You will learn all the programming essentials to start creating your own VBA code from scratch.

Excel 2019 Macros and VBA will enable you to create solutions that will save you time and effort, create consistency in your work, and help to minimize errors in your Excel projects.

For more details go to:
https://www.excelbytes.com/excel-books

Made in the USA
Monee, IL
24 January 2021